The STARTUPRENEUR
Practical Playbook for a Successful Startup

DR. SANJEEV PATNI

FOREWORD BY
DR. CHINTAN VAISHNAV

Mission Director
Atal Innovation Mission
NITI Aayog, Government of India

INDIA • SINGAPORE • MALAYSIA

ISBN
Paperback 979-8-89519-812-4
Hardcase 979-8-89556-258-1

CONTENTS

FOREWORD

DR. CHINTAN VAISHNAV

Mission Director
Atal Innovation Mission
NITI Aayog
Government of India
New Delhi. INDIA

'THE STARTUPRENEUR' comes at an important time when many talented Indians are considering launching a startup. At the minimum, the book ought to impress upon them the vast array of decisions they will have to navigate as a startup founder. Of course, it is these decisions that make the journey of building a startup an exhilarating one. Such decisions are also the reason a founder of a startup grows, irrespective of the fate of the enterprise. The book is a grand survey of many such decisions.

Fortunately, the book comes at a juncture when there is much support for startups to succeed in India. As catalogued here, the startup ecosystem today offers the necessary infrastructure, mentorship, investment, markets, and policy protection. At present, India has the third-largest Startup Ecosystem in the world, with over 125,000 startups and 100 Unicorns with over 1 Billion USD valuation. Even so, a startup's journey is inherently risky.

Reading this book should provide a startup with a "long view" of the nature of this risk along the various stages of its journey. One difference between a rookie entrepreneur and a seasoned entrepreneur is the latter's ability to foresee risks and build in measures to forestall or mitigate them. Doing so is difficult for first-time entrepreneurs because they have not experienced the full spectrum yet. For example, in a typical tech startup, mitigating the technical or scientific risk takes much of the attention of the entrepreneur at an early stage, often the neglect of attention necessary to market research, careful selection of investors, or building a strong team. Paying attention to the advice in this book will force a more balanced approach, which otherwise would be seen only by someone who has experienced failures.

Hundreds of books today advise startups. Unique to this book is the focus on many behavioural factors such as the mindset and attitude of a founder, determining who makes a good co-founder, identifying the right persona for building a strong team, looking for the right type of investors, using contractual means to avoid potential disputes and resolving them if they do arise, and more. These aspects involve paying close attention to human factors and making difficult choices about them that are ultimately as important, if not more so, as the popular advice given to entrepreneurs, such as having a strong product-market fit or a viable business model. A startup that does not pay equal attention to the human dimension is a time bomb waiting to explode, leading to its disintegration. This book can surely help founders avert such a mistake.

Any opinion about a book is credible only when one combines knowledge of what it says with an understanding of who is saying it. The good news is that the advice in this book comes from Dr. Sanjeev Patni, a seasoned professional, successful entrepreneur, and someone actively building India's startup ecosystem. Allow me to share the circumstances under which I first met Dr. Patni that give me the confidence to say so.

It was April 15, 2021, when I took charge as the Mission Director, Atal Innovation Mission, Niti Aayog, the flagship initiative of the Government of India to build a culture of innovation and entrepreneurship across the length and breadth of our nation. This was an acrimonious time, as the very next day after my joining, India declared the second lockdown to combat the onset of the deadly Delta variant of Covid-19. I was immediately asked to join the Government of India's Covid Task Force. It was time for intense firefighting in order to save many lives as our nation literally gasped for oxygen.

Being the innovation lead, many new ideas and claims for tackling various situations were directed at me. Amidst this frenzy came a young man from IIT Kanpur who proposed that we could perhaps administer medical oxygen to a Covid-19 patient from a Liquid Propulsion Gas (LPG) cylinder. The idea had an instant appeal because our nation has a large spare capacity for manufacturing LPG cylinders as well as a nationwide supply chain set up for taking cylinders to any corner. The only wrinkle was that we had never used the LPG cylinder for oxygen, as its primary use was for supplying cooking fuel. The young man's claim needed some aggressive experimentation.

I started to knock on many doors to see who could support such an experiment. Some chemical engineering experts engaged in designing the experiment, but we had little luck finding someone willing to conduct the experiment. The large oil and gas companies in India's Public Sector too initially brushed us aside. In these moments, our team introduced me to Dr. Patni, saying he may have both the enterprise and resources to engage, as he is the CEO of the Atal Incubation Centre Prestige in Indore. They were right!

In the days to come, Sanjeev and I engaged in administering oxygen via an LPG cylinder to demonstrate that a patient who needed a 3-5 litre per minute flow could survive on such a system for 3-5 hours. It was Sanjeev who got us to this point. He roped in Dipin Jain, a brilliant engineer at Prestige, to try out the idea. He even convinced his mother, who was a patient using an external oxygen cylinder anyway, to try out our system. We had the first glimpse of something that could be a breakthrough if we could validate the idea through the standards body to ensure that it was safe on a large scale.

In the process, I learned that Sanjeev is a successful serial entrepreneur who has built and sold companies before, that his efforts have contributed to making Indore, Madhya Pradesh, a vibrant startup hub of central India, and that he has made AIC Prestige a hub for entrepreneurship in areas such as Software as a Service (SaaS), Drones, and more recently, taken on futuristic topics like Quantum Computing. This book brings to you his rich and diverse experience.

Dr. Chintan Vaishnav

New Delhi, India

REVIEWS

Embark on a Thrilling Startup Adventure with *The Startupreneur*

As an entrepreneur and a second-generation business owner in my family, I have personally experienced the transformative potential of innovation and the unwavering determination that drives successful endeavours. Starting a business is akin to sailing across unknown waters; besides having a great concept, you also need to have good timing and the courage to take calculated risks. Dr. Sanjeev Patni's book *The Startupreneur*, which offers invaluable insights into the startup sector, perfectly encapsulates the essence of this experience.

Starting a business is an expedition into the unknown with high stakes and potentially enormous rewards. It is not just about creating a business; in the startup ecosystem, exponential growth goes beyond basic expansion. It involves cultivating a culture that is adaptable, creative, and always evolving. Such growth requires a deep understanding of market dynamics, the ability to swiftly respond to customer needs, and the willingness to embrace change as an inevitable and essential part of success.

Dr. Patni skillfully narrates gripping tales of startups that have defied expectations, achieved rapid growth, and significantly impacted their industries. As readers traverse the pages of this book, they will explore the strategies that propelled these ventures forward and gain priceless insights from their experiences. These narratives are not just about success; they are about the relentless pursuit of excellence and the audacity to dream big.

The Startupreneur is a treasure trove of knowledge for aspiring entrepreneurs, seasoned business leaders, and anyone interested in the dynamics of startup culture. It delves into the importance of fostering a culture of innovation and agility, one that continuously adapts to a dynamic marketplace. The book emphasises the critical role of monitoring market trends, swiftly responding to customer needs, and viewing change as an essential element of growth.

The Startupreneur invites you to explore the world of startups and the individuals who drive exponential growth through their brilliant judgement and unwavering determination. The stories within are not just tales of success but also examples of visionary entrepreneurs redefining industries. Dive into these pages and draw inspiration from the phenomenal journeys of these entrepreneurs. Let these tales fuel your aspirations and reinforce your belief in the creative potential within each of us.

May this book be a beacon of inspiration, igniting your startup dreams and solidifying your conviction in the power of innovation and entrepreneurship?

Dr. Davish Jain

Chairman, Prestige Education Foundation | Chancellor, Prestige University | President, Prestige Group of Industries | Author

***

The Startupreneur by Dr. Sanjeev Patni is a valuable resource for aspiring entrepreneurs. The book offers practical advice, covering all aspects of starting and growing a startup. From idea generation to funding, marketing, and scaling, it is a comprehensive guide for navigating the startup world.

It provides valuable advice on the founder's characteristics and the pitfalls that determine whether a startup succeeds or fails. Dr. Patni ensures the content is simple, clear, and offers actionable insights to make complex concepts accessible to readers at any experience level.

The book is an essential read for anyone serious about launching or refining a startup.

Sam Pitroda

Scientist with 100+ global patents | Author

***

Over the last two decades, I've had the privilege of witnessing the dynamic evolution of India's startup ecosystem. A founders' journey to success is almost always full of hurdles, and any resources and tools which make their journeys as frictionless as possible are highly valuable.

Dr. Sanjeev Patni's latest work, *The Startupreneur*, has all the right ingredients to serve as a comprehensive playbook for startup founders, encapsulating the essence of transforming a simple idea into a thriving enterprise. Dr. Patni meticulously guides readers through every stage of the startup lifecycle—from the initial spark of ideation to the complexities of market research, team building, and scaling operations.

What sets this book apart is its practical approach, blending actionable insights with real-world applications that resonate with today's dynamic startup environment.

One of the book's greatest strengths is its relevance to the Indian startup ecosystem. Dr. Patni addresses the unique challenges and opportunities faced by Indian entrepreneurs, providing valuable insights tailored to the local context.

This is a highly recommended read for any aspiring founder.

Subrata Mitra

Partner at Accel (Venture Capital firm)

*****

If you wish to be an entrepreneur or are even remotely considering starting something of your own, do read this book. My dear friend Sanjeev has poured his extensive wisdom over the years into succinctly explaining the start, the challenges and pitfalls, and the fundraising strategies that a Startupreneur will face. He also elucidates techniques to mitigate them.

He has touched upon the importance of courage to step into this world, and the balance needed to tide over risks. I highly recommend this book. Best of luck to Sanjeev and to his readers as they embark upon a new journey.

Nikhil Malhotra

Chief Innovation Officer | Head of Emerging Tech | WEF AI & Quantum Fellow | Tech Mahindra.

*****

This book on the subject of entrepreneurship is competently authored by Mr. Sanjeev Patni.

It comprehensively covers:

a. Diverse topics ranging from the idea stage up to fundraising, including important subjects like the startup mindset, reasons for failure, team building, go-to-market strategy options, etc.

b. Various hurdles entrepreneurs may encounter on their startup journeys and their plausible solutions.

I hope this book will serve as an encyclopaedia for innovators looking to commence their journey as entrepreneurs and scale their startups sustainably in the long term.

My sincere compliments to Dr. Sanjeev Patni, who has spared his valuable time in elucidating all the important ecosystems pertaining to startups under one roof and simplifying the startup journey for all entrepreneurs.

Paresh P. Shah

P. P. Shah and Associates, Mumbai

***

A most comprehensive playbook for venturing and accelerating the journey towards building a successful startup. Dr. Patni provides a complete blueprint of what works and what pitfalls to avoid while navigating your journey. The book discusses each aspect of building a business, organisation, market, team, and the resources needed and available for entrepreneurs, based on practical experiences and not just theoretical concepts.

The Startupreneur also provides links to essential resources for efficiently navigating the journey of being an entrepreneur. This is a book that is a must-read for anyone who is thinking of ever getting into building their startup.

Dr. Satyam Priyadarshy

CEO, ReigniteFuture, USA | Quantum Computing Scientist

***

Dr. Sanjeev Patni has encapsulated his entrepreneurial journey experience over 25 years into a set of practical skills that can be learnt by aspirational entrepreneurs embarking upon their careers and journeys.

Dr. Chandra Patni

CEO, HCE Services Limited, London | Serial entrepreneur

***

Following the footsteps of the "Lean Startup" methodology, *The Startupreneur* by Dr. Sanjeev Patni makes one of the most important points of entrepreneurial success: Get started. Follow a methodology. Have a long-term vision. After 20 years in startups as a five-time founder, investor, and mentor at Techstars & the German Accelerator NYC, I have seen countless ambitious entrepreneurs getting lost in sales decks, investor pitches, product design, and false promises. Focus on a smart strategy, execute a diligent plan, and you will go far. *The Startupreneur* is the perfect book to show you the way. Being a founder is one of life's ultimate rewards. I hope this book will inspire you to take that leap of faith.

André M. König

CEO, Global Quantum Intelligence, NYC & London

***

The Startupreneur by Dr. Sanjeev Patni is a must-read for anyone looking to start or grow a business. This guide walks entrepreneurs through every step, from idea to scaling, offering practical advice to tackle common challenges. Whether you're new to the startup world or have experience, Dr. Patni's clear strategies for managing risks and driving growth make this book an invaluable resource. It's highly recommended for anyone eager to turn their startup vision into reality.

Pramit Maakoday

Cofounder & Director, Boston Center of Excellence for Health and Development, USA| Investor

***

The Startupreneur is an invaluable resource for anyone embarking on the startup journey. The author, Dr. Sanjeev Patni, provides a thorough blueprint, highlighting effective strategies and potential pitfalls in building a successful startup. The book covers every crucial aspect of entrepreneurship drawing from real-world experience rather than just theory.

It includes links to key resources that can help startup founders to navigate their path more efficiently. It also details the entire entrepreneurial process, from the initial idea to securing funding, and tackles critical topics such as the startup mindset, reasons for failure, team building, and go-to-market strategies. It discusses the challenges entrepreneurs may encounter and offers practical solutions.

I am confident that *The Startuprenuer* will become a trusted reference for innovators looking to launch and grow their businesses sustainably. My heartfelt thanks to Dr. Sanjeev Patni for his dedication in clarifying the complexities of the startup ecosystem and making the entrepreneurial journey more accessible to aspiring founders.

For anyone considering starting their own company, reading this book is essential.

Jay Jain

President, TiE MP | Investor | Serial entrepreneur

***

ACKNOWLEDGEMENTS

The insights and perspectives in this book are drawn from my experiences and interactions, which have been profoundly enlightening.

I am deeply grateful to Dr. Chintan Vaishnav (Mission Director, Atal Innovation Mission) for his unwavering support and guidance in writing this book. His broad global outlook and experience at esteemed institutions like MIT have been valuable in conceptualising this book.

I extend my heartfelt thanks to Dr. Davish Jain (Chairman of Prestige Group) for his constant inspiration, belief, and insightful suggestions. His candid viewpoints were pivotal to the development of this book, and I hold him in the highest regard.

My sincere thanks to my esteemed friends and colleagues for their inspiration, learning, support and guidance at various stages and in writing this book.

Finally, I express my deepest gratitude to my dear family and my gang-of-friends, of whom I am very proud and who have been steadfast in their support through life's ebb and flow. I take their unwavering support almost for granted and immensely cherish their presence and participation in all walks of life.

Dr. Sanjeev Patni

PREFACE

Not too long ago, while students were stepping out of college, there were a handful of options, each seeming somewhat predictable. One could take up a job, dive into the family business, or perhaps join the business of someone known.

Starting a business was then often discouraged and warned of as an uphill struggle—juggling finances, wrestling with bureaucratic hurdles, chasing customers and then payments, hastily assembling a team, and navigating the nightmare of logistics. Success felt like it hinged on the mercy of government approvals, banks, or the network of family ties.

Fast forward to today, and the narrative has been completely rewritten. There is this game-changing phenomenon shaking things up—the startup revolution—the third option. It is not just about clocking in and out; it is about forging something entirely new. What is even more exhilarating is that it is no longer a fringe pursuit; startups are grabbing the spotlight and have become a formidable preference.

Discovering that someone your age, right in your own city, has successfully started a startup can be incredibly uplifting. It is a powerful reminder that dreams can become reality and success is achievable, even for people just like you. Rather than feeling envious, let their accomplishment serve as a motivation boost. It is a wake-up call that your goals are within reach, and with determination and effort, you can make your own dreams come true. Embrace the inspiration, and let it fuel your drive to explore your own entrepreneurial journey. You never know—you could be the next success story that inspires someone else in your community!

Now, let us throw in a dose of reality for hard work: For every startup that soars to success, there are probably nine that hit roadblocks, and, unfortunately, most of these startups do not make it. Why? Well, the road to startup triumph is riddled with pitfalls—missteps in strategy, financial turbulence, team dynamics, and the relentless pressure of competition.

Many startups stumble and fall, not due to a lack of passion or a shortage of brilliant ideas, but often because they are not aware of the requirements of following methodologies detailed in this book, and thus entrepreneurs are caught off-guard by the challenges they face during their entrepreneurial journey.

Entrepreneurs may be born with talent, drive, and energy to focus on a single-minded goal or business objective, but the methodology to follow needs to be learned—hopefully through insights from this book rather than from multiple startup failures along the route to eventual business success.

This book is a practical playbook that dissects the common pitfalls, offering insights and strategies to navigate the treacherous terrain. I will delve into why startups often stumble and, more importantly, how you can gracefully exit the entrepreneurial journey, as well as sometimes learn from those pitfalls to pivot and improve your odds of success.

In this book, you will embark on a rollercoaster ride through the unpredictable, electrifying world of startups. From the first spark of an idea to the adrenaline-pumping pursuit of funding, the whirlwind of scaling up, and the adrenaline-charged face-off with competition—this journey is nothing short of a thrilling adventure. This is not just a guide; it is an enthusiastic rallying cry fuelled by stories, wisdom from those who have tasted both victory and setbacks and real-life examples that will spark the imagination of anyone itching to explore the startup galaxy.

This book is an invitation to the most exciting, challenging, and fulfilling ride of your work life. I am not just uncovering the secrets of startups; I am ushering you into a league where audacity, resilience, and vision collide to redefine the future of business. It is not just a story; it is a call to join those who dare to dream big and shape a world where innovation knows no bounds. Get ready to turn the page, and let the adventure begin.

The pages ahead are not a one-size-fits-all manual because the path to startup success is as diverse as the individuals who embark upon it. It requires a spirit that thrives in working methodically to eliminate ambiguity, a mindset that welcomes challenges as opportunities, and a determination that refuses to yield in the face of setbacks.

So, as we navigate the exhilarating landscape of startups in the pages ahead, remember that this journey demands more than just business acumen—it requires the kind of personal courage, resilience, risk-taking attitude, and self-belief that transforms dreams into reality.

If you resonate with these qualities, then the adventure of a startup may just be the perfect canvas for your aspirations. Embrace the challenge, and let us forge ahead on a journey that promises not only financial rewards but a sense of accomplishment that transcends the confines of a traditional career. Embrace the challenges, relish the victories, recognise and pivot around the roadblocks, and let the startup adventure become a source of lasting pride and personal satisfaction.

Startups can defy expectations and achieve meteoric success, creating ripples of innovation and transforming industries. These success stories are not just about luck; they are often a result of ingenious strategies, agile decision-making, and an unyielding commitment to a groundbreaking vision. Startups like these do not merely inch forward; they leapfrog, challenging the status quo and reshaping the competitive landscape.

The secret sauce lies in their ability to identify and seize opportunities with unparalleled agility. Whether it is leveraging cutting-edge technologies, tapping into emerging markets, or redefining business models, these startups have an innate sense of timing and an audacious willingness to take calculated risks.

Exponential growth, in the context of startups, is not just about expanding in scale but about developing a culture of innovation and adaptability. It involves staying attuned to market dynamics, swiftly responding to customer needs, and embracing change as an inherent part of the journey.

In the pages ahead, we will unravel the stories of startups that defied conventional wisdom, rapidly scaled their operations, and left an indelible mark on their respective industries. We will explore the strategies that propelled them forward and the lessons that can be gleaned from their experiences. The aim is not just to marvel at their achievements but to distil actionable insights that aspiring entrepreneurs can apply to their own endeavours.

So, buckle up for a ride through the dynamic world of startups, where exponential growth isn't just a goal; it is a testament to the transformative power of bold ideas, strategic thinking, and the unwavering spirit of those who dare to dream big. Get ready to be inspired by the stories of startups that didn't just make it—they redefined the game.

As you venture forth, remember that success is not just about avoiding failure; it is about embracing it as part of the journey. This book is not promising a magic formula, but it is offering you a map, a compass, a flashlight, and a survival guide rolled into one. So, buckle up, absorb the wisdom within these pages, and get ready to chart a course that not only acknowledges the risks but transforms them into stepping stones towards your own entrepreneurial triumph.

George Bernard Shaw said, **"The reasonable man adapts himself to the world: the unreasonable one persists in trying to adapt the world to himself. Therefore, all progress depends on the unreasonable man."**

Be ready to be that unreasonable man and welcome to the adventure!

STARTUP TERMINOLOGY

Understanding the terminology prevailing in the domain is essential for anyone involved in the startup ecosystem. It provides a common language for discussing strategies, challenges, and opportunities, enabling effective communication and collaboration among founders, investors, and other stakeholders.

Angel Investor

An angel investor is an individual who provides financial backing to startups, typically in exchange for ownership equity or convertible debt. Angels often invest during the early stages when startups are too risky for traditional investors. Examples include Peter Thiel, who famously invested in Facebook during its early days. They often offer not just capital but also mentorship and industry connections. For example, Mohandas Pai and Indian Angel Network.

Bootstrapping

Bootstrapping involves funding a startup using personal savings, revenue from early sales, or other non-traditional methods instead of seeking external investment. Bootstrapped startups retain full ownership and control but may face slower growth due to limited resources.

Burn Rate

Burn rate refers to the rate at which a startup is spending its available cash over a specific period, typically monthly. It is a crucial metric for assessing financial health and runway—the time until a startup runs out of money. High burn rates can be unsustainable without corresponding revenue growth.

Cap Table (Capitalisation Table)

A cap table is a spreadsheet or document that outlines the ownership structure of a company, including equity ownership, option grants, convertible securities, and other securities. It provides a snapshot of who owns what percentage of the company and is crucial for understanding ownership dynamics, valuation, and potential dilution.

Disruption

Disruption refers to the process by which a new product or service fundamentally changes the existing market or industry, often displacing established players. Startups that disrupt industries typically offer innovative solutions that challenge traditional business models. For example, Netflix disrupted the DVD rental industry by introducing online streaming, fundamentally changing how people consume entertainment.

Due Diligence

Due diligence is the process of investigating and evaluating a startup's business, financial, legal, and operational aspects before making an investment or entering into a business transaction. It is essential for investors to thoroughly assess the risks and opportunities associated with a potential investment.

Equity

Equity represents ownership in a company. Startups typically offer equity to founders, employees, and investors in exchange for capital, labour, or other contributions. Equity can be diluted over time as new investors are brought in or additional shares are issued through stock options or grants.

Exit Strategy

An exit strategy outlines how founders and investors plan to cash out their investment in a startup. Common exit strategies include acquisition by a larger company, initial public offering (IPO), or management buyout. Having a clear exit strategy is essential for investors to understand how they will eventually cash out their investment.

MVP (Minimum Viable Product/Proposition)

The MVP is the most basic version of a product or service proposition that allows a startup to test its core hypothesis with the least effort. It typically includes only essential features, allowing the team to gather feedback from early users and iterate. For example, Airbnb's MVP was a simple website that allowed users to rent out an air mattress in their living room.

Pitch Deck

A pitch deck is a presentation, usually in slide format, used by startups to pitch their business idea or investment opportunity to potential investors. It typically includes information about the problem being solved; the solution offered market opportunity, business model, traction, team, and financial projections. A well-crafted pitch deck is essential for attracting investment.

Pivot

A pivot involves changing the fundamental direction of a startup in response to feedback or market conditions. Startups often pivot to find a more promising product-market fit or to address a new opportunity. Instagram, originally a location-based social network, pivoted to become a photo-sharing platform when they realised users were most engaged with that feature.

Run Rate

The run rate refers to a company's annualised revenue based on its current performance over a shorter period, such as a month or a quarter. It is often used as a projection of future revenue and growth. For example, if a company generates $1 million in revenue in the first quarter, its run rate would be $4 million annually.

Runway

The runway is the amount of time a startup has until it exhausts its cash reserves based on its current burn rate. It is a critical factor in fundraising and strategic planning. For instance, if a startup has $500,000 in the bank and a burn rate of $50,000 per month, its runway is 10 months.

Scalability

Scalability refers to a startup's ability to handle growth in users, customers, or workload without compromising performance or increasing costs proportionally. Scalable businesses can expand their operations efficiently as demand increases. For example, software-as-a-service (SaaS) companies like Salesforce can onboard thousands of new customers without significantly increasing their infrastructure costs.

Seed Round

A seed round is the initial funding round for a startup, usually raised from friends, family, and angel investors. It is used to validate the business idea, build a prototype, and conduct early market testing. Seed rounds typically precede larger funding rounds such as Series A, B, and C.

Series A, B, C, etc.

Series A, B, C, and so forth refer to successive rounds of financing that startups raise as they grow and mature. Each round typically involves larger investment amounts and is used to scale the business, expand operations, and accelerate growth. Series A rounds are usually the first institutional funding rounds, led by venture capital firms, following the seed round.

Term Sheet

A term sheet is a non-binding document outlining the key terms and conditions of an investment or acquisition agreement between a startup and an investor or acquirer. It typically includes details such as valuation, investment amount, equity ownership, rights and preferences of preferred stock, and other terms of the deal. Term sheets serve as a basis for negotiating the final agreement.

Unicorn

A unicorn is a startup valued at over $1 billion. Achieving unicorn status is a significant milestone and often indicates rapid growth and disruptive potential. Examples include Uber, Airbnb, and SpaceX.

Valuation

Valuation is the process of determining the financial value of a startup or business. It is crucial for fundraising, acquisitions, and other financial transactions. Valuation methods vary but often involve assessing the company's revenue, growth potential, market size, competitive landscape, and comparable transactions.

Venture Capital (VC)

Venture capital refers to funding provided by investment firms to startups and small businesses with high-growth potential. VCs typically invest larger sums in exchange for equity stakes and actively support portfolio companies with expertise and networking opportunities. Examples of prominent VC firms include Sequoia Capital, Chiratae Ventures, and Accel Venture Partners.

Vesting

Vesting refers to the process by which employees earn ownership of their equity stake in a company over time, usually through a predetermined schedule. It is a common practice to incentivise employees to stay with the company and align their interests with its long-term success. For example, an employee might have a four-year vesting schedule with a one-year cliff, meaning they earn 25% of their equity after one year, and the rest vest monthly over the next 3 years.

THE STARTUP ECOSYSTEM

In this chapter, the definition of a startup according to Indian regulatory norms is given. It is essential, at the outset of the startup journey, for the lead founder to build a strong co-founding team, without which there is no chance of success. On the startup tollgate journey, founders will meet with challenges, pitfalls, excitement, achievements, failures, and hopefully financial rewards.

SUCCESSFUL STARTUP DEFINITION

A startup is a young company that is developing or has developed a unique product or service and is bringing the product or service to market. Successful startups are typically characterised by their innovative, nimble business model, disruptive technology, and unique value proposition, which can EXPONENTIALLY SCALE in a short span of time.

In India, according to the Department for Promotion of Industry and Internal Trade (DPIIT), Ministry of Commerce and Industry, Government of India, an entity is considered a startup only if it meets the following criteria:

1. Up to 10 years from the date of its incorporation/registration.

2. If it is incorporated as a private limited company (as defined in the Companies Act, 2013) or registered as a partnership firm (under section 59 of the Partnership Act, 1932) or a limited liability partnership (under the Limited Liability Partnership Act, 2008) in India.

3. Turnover of the entity for any of the financial years since its incorporation/registration has not exceeded INR 100 crore.

4. Entity is working towards innovation, development, deployment, or commercialisation of new products, processes, or services driven by technology or intellectual property.

5. The business model of the entity is scalable and has the potential to generate significant employment or create wealth.

This definition is important because startups meeting these criteria are eligible for various benefits under the Startup India initiative launched by the Government of India and the state governments.

STARTUP IS A BUSINESS WITH A HUGE PASSION

Rajesh is very passionate, a great cook, and wants to develop a healthy food startup based on a cloud kitchen. He is very talented, and his preparations are appreciated by all.

Let me ask you—do you think by being a good cook his startup can be successful?

The right answer is—yes, but provided only if he has business acumen and properly understands the concepts of business and marketing.

Founders must:

- Have a huge passion for the business mission and practical business acumen.

- Demonstrate resilience, patience, alignment, passion, conviction, and extreme motivation.

- Stay inspired, learning from success stories and role models.

- Be prepared to pivot or exit the startup journey reluctantly, but gracefully.

Strategic Vision: Balancing Passion with People Skills

Passion fuels the startup's engine, but strategic vision steers its course. As a founder, you will be required to strike a delicate balance between passion and pragmatism. You have to understand when to dive headfirst into the excitement of your vision and when to pause, evaluate, and adjust your strategies based on the ever-changing business landscape.

To the passionate co-founders embarking on the exhilarating journey of a startup, it is crucial to recognise that while passion fuels the engine, understanding the intricacies of business is the roadmap to sustainable success.

The passion and vision that drive you to initiate a startup are undoubtedly the driving forces, but to navigate the ever-evolving business landscape, it is essential to equip yourself with a diverse skill set. In the entrepreneurial world, people skills are as vital as any technical know-how.

Founders must master the art of assembling, motivating, and leading a team. Effective communication, empathetic leadership, and the ability to develop a collaborative culture are the cornerstones of a thriving startup team. Your passion can inspire, but your people skills will determine how well that inspiration translates into collective action.

Long-term Sustainable Profit, Understanding Customers and Competition

Being business-savvy extends beyond the confines of your product or service. It involves understanding your customers' needs and behaviour. Passionate co-founders should delve into market research, studying trends, analysing consumer preferences, and keeping a watchful eye on the competition. This knowledge is the compass guiding your business decisions and steering your startup towards uncharted territories.

Amid the excitement of launching a startup, it is paramount for passionate co-founders to ingrain a fundamental truth—the prime purpose of any business is profit. While the initial impetus often stems from a desire to make a difference or solve a problem, sustainability hinges on financial viability. Profit is not a mere outcome; it is the lifeblood that fuels growth, innovation, and the ability to make a lasting impact.

Understanding the nuances of profit, from optimising revenue streams to managing expenses judiciously, forms the bedrock of a resilient business. It provides the means to reinvest, expand, and, most importantly, fulfil the visionary goals that ignited the entrepreneurial spark in the first place. Passion may set the stage, but long-term profitability ensures the show goes on, underscoring the indispensable role of financial success in realising the broader long-term goals and aspirations of a startup.

Financial Prudence is the Startup's Base Foundation

Passion ignites the spark, but a successful startup requires more than just enthusiasm. It demands a solid understanding of fundamental business principles. Accounting, often considered the language of business, is the first checkpoint. Estimating costs and creating realistic budgets is critical for sustainability. Knowing how to calculate costs, set pricing strategies, estimate sales pipelines and conversion rates, and manage resources ensures that your passion project thrives and grows over the long haul. Budgeting monthly cashflows provides insights into strategic financial planning, helping founders make judicious resource choices that balance ambition with financial prudence.

LIFE OF A STARTUP FOUNDER

As you embark upon your journey as a startup founder, it is important to know what the life of a founder is like. In achieving your dream and aspiration, there are challenges, excitement, fun, and reward.

Challenges - Financial Strain, Uncertainty, and Risk

As a startup founder, you are likely to encounter numerous challenges along the journey of building your business, from uncertainty and risk of the business model to financial strain, all while trying to maintain a work-life balance.

Startups often operate on tight budgets, and as a co-founder, you may face significant financial challenges. Securing funding is a constant concern, as it is essential for covering initial setup costs, hiring talent, and scaling operations. Managing cash flow becomes crucial, as any misstep could threaten the sustainability of the business. Whether it is bootstrapping, seeking investment from friends and family, angels, venture capitalists, or crowdfunding, founders generally must continuously seek sources of funding to fuel their growth.

The startup journey is inherently uncertain, with risks at every turn. Navigating through uncertainties, market fluctuations, and unexpected obstacles requires resilience and adaptability. Founders must learn to embrace uncertainty and make decisions in the face of ambiguity. Market conditions can change rapidly, and unexpected challenges can arise at any moment. Whether it is dealing with changing consumer preferences, technological advancements, or regulatory changes, startup founders must remain agile and pivot when necessary to stay ahead.

Work-Life Balance

Founders often find themselves fully immersed in their work, blurring the lines between personal and professional life. Building a startup is a demanding and time-consuming endeavour, and achieving a balance becomes a constant challenge. Support from your family in your endeavours is a prerequisite for potential success.

The pressure to succeed can take a toll on one's personal life, leading to increased stress and burnout. It is not uncommon for founders to work long hours, sacrificing personal time and relationships for the success of their business.

However, maintaining a healthy work-life balance is essential for long-term success and overall well-being. Finding ways to prioritise self-care, set boundaries, and delegate tasks can help co-founders avoid burnout and maintain their health and happiness.

STARTUP MINDSET

Raising a startup is hard at the beginning, bumpy in the middle, and gorgeous when successful. It needs a typical mindset, which is strong in conviction and willpower, resilient, passionate, has a high quotient for risk-taking, and has no plan B.

You can test yourself with some simple tests.

Story of the Man Lost in a Desert

A man, lost in a hot desert, keeps walking. His water container runs out of water; he is totally parched and about to die. Just then, he sees some habitat in the distance. As a last hope, he collects all his strength to reach there, only to find that there is no one there. He finds a hand pump (like in villages), but it gives no water. He finds a bottle of water there, with a note—if you pour this water into the hole in the hand pump, then it will start to give water.

He thinks—if I drink this water, I will survive for some more time, and then maybe I will find some help. Then he thinks—if this hand pump starts to work, then I can drink as much water as I want and refill the water container, which will help me survive for longer.

The question you should ask yourself is: 'What would you have done in such a situation?'

Drink the bottle of water; or take the risk of pouring the water from the bottle into the hand pump, expecting it to start?

Let us have another test:

Two paths lead to a destination. The longer path is a well-built, straight road. The shorter path is less travelled, goes through a beautiful forest and waterfalls, but is full of perils. Which one would you take?

    a. Straight road

    b. Forest Route

If your honest answer for both is the latter, then you are a typical entrepreneur and a startup founder who would take chances and risks and enjoy the journey to reach the goal.

Welcome to the party of startup founders!!

Embrace the Passion for Your Idea

As a founder, the journey of turning an idea into a successful startup is one that demands unwavering commitment, boundless creativity, and the ability to inspire others. However, amidst the challenges and uncertainties that come with building a business from scratch, there is one indispensable element that serves as the cornerstone of success: passion.

Passion is more than just a fleeting feeling; it is the intrinsic drive that propels founders forward, even in the face of seemingly insurmountable obstacles. When you are deeply passionate about your startup idea, it becomes more than just a business venture—it becomes a mission, a purpose that fuels your every action and decision.

Driving Commitment and Creativity

Passion is the driving force behind your commitment to your startup. It gives you the resilience to weather the storms that inevitably come your way. When you're passionate about your idea, you're more likely to persevere through the toughest challenges and find creative solutions to problems.

Your passion pushes you to constantly innovate and refine your approach, ensuring that you never settle for mediocrity.

Fuelling Perseverance

Building a startup is not for the faint of heart. There will be countless setbacks, rejections, and failures along the way. However, it is your passion for your idea that will give you the strength to persevere, even when the odds are stacked against you. Passion fuels your determination to keep going, even when others might have given up.

Maintaining Enthusiasm for Long-Term Success

The journey of building a successful startup is a marathon, not a sprint. It requires sustained enthusiasm and energy over the long haul. When you are deeply passionate about your idea, you naturally exude enthusiasm and optimism, which are infectious qualities that attract others to your cause. Your passion becomes a magnet, drawing like-minded individuals who share your vision and are inspired by your mission.

Embracing the passion for your idea is not just about personal fulfilment; it is also a strategic advantage that can set your startup on the path to long-term success. When you are truly passionate about what you're building, you inspire others to believe in your vision, and together, you can overcome any obstacle that stands in your way.

Developing a Resilient Attitude in the Face of Challenges

There are two boxers in a ring; one is lean-thin-agile, and the other is strong and heavyweight. The question to you is—*who will win?*

Most will think that the heavyweight boxer will win. But, if the lean-thin-agile boxer decides to fight with the belief and conviction that he will die but not leave the ring until he defeats the heavyweight, he is then sure to win.

Time and again, we have seen this happen. In sports and wars, the fragile have won over the mighty owing to their attitude, belief, and never-look-back attitude.

The Power of Conviction, Determination, and Resilience

In the world of startups and entrepreneurship, where uncertainty is the only certainty, resilience stands as the cornerstone of success. It is the ability to view challenges not as insurmountable obstacles but as opportunities for growth and development. A resilient mindset empowers founders to bounce back from setbacks, learn from failures, and navigate the unpredictable journey of building a startup with composure.

Embracing Challenges as Opportunities

In the realm of entrepreneurship and startups, challenges are not roadblocks but stepping stones. A resilient mindset allows founders to embrace these challenges as inherent to the entrepreneurial process. Instead of being deterred by difficulties, they adapt, innovate, and maintain a forward-looking perspective even in the face of adversity. Every setback becomes a chance to learn, grow, and improve. This ability to adapt and innovate is what sets successful entrepreneurs apart.

Navigating the Unpredictable Journey

The journey of building a startup is filled with twists and turns, ups and downs. A resilient mindset allows founders to navigate this journey with composure. It enables them to stay focused on their goals, even when faced with uncertainty and adversity. Instead of being overwhelmed by challenges, they see them as opportunities for growth and development. In this way, resilience becomes not just a trait but a guiding principle, empowering founders to overcome obstacles and achieve their dreams.

Learning from Failure

Failure is an inevitable part of the entrepreneurial journey. However, it is not the failure itself but the response to it that determines the future of a startup. Resilience enables founders to learn from their failures, iterate on their ideas, and emerge stronger and more determined. It is this ability to bounce back from failure that allows startups to ultimately succeed.

Aligning Personal Aspirations with Startup Objectives

As a founder, it is essential to align your personal values, passions, and aspirations with the broader objectives of your startup. This alignment ensures a sense of purpose and authenticity, contributing to a more fulfilling and sustainable entrepreneurial journey.

Finding Purpose

When personal and startup goals are harmonised, founders are more likely to find meaning and fulfilment in their work. They are driven not just by the desire for success but by a deeper sense of purpose. This sense of purpose fuels their determination and resilience, enabling them to overcome challenges and stay focused on their goals.

Staying Authentic

Authenticity is key to building trust and credibility, both with customers and with investors. When founders are aligned with their startup's objectives, they are more likely to stay true to their values and beliefs. This authenticity not only attracts customers and investors but also helps to build a strong and loyal team.

Building a Sustainable Business

Ultimately, aligning personal aspirations with startup objectives leads to a more sustainable business. When founders are passionate about what they do and believe in the mission of their startup, they are more likely to weather the inevitable ups and downs of entrepreneurship. They are driven not just by the desire for financial success but by a deeper sense of purpose and meaning.

Creating a Roadmap for Short-term and Long-term Success

Establishing a comprehensive roadmap is essential for providing a strategic guide for achieving both short-term milestones and long-term objectives.

Setting Clear Goals

The first step in creating a roadmap for success is to set clear and achievable goals. These goals should be specific, measurable, and time-bound, allowing founders to track their progress and make adjustments as needed.

Anticipating Challenges

Entrepreneurship is full of surprises, and challenges are bound to arise along the way. A comprehensive roadmap allows founders to anticipate these challenges and prepare for them in advance. By identifying potential obstacles and developing strategies for overcoming them, founders can minimise their impact on the success of their startup.

Adapting Strategies

The business landscape is constantly evolving, and what works today may not work tomorrow. A dynamic roadmap allows founders to adapt their strategies in response to changes in the market and the competitive landscape. By regularly revisiting and refining their roadmap, founders can ensure that it remains aligned with the evolving needs of their startup and the ever-changing business environment.

Overcoming Founder's Burnout

Recognising signs of burnout and stress is crucial for your well-being as an entrepreneur, as it allows you to implement proactive strategies to prevent and overcome burnout. Strategies for maintaining mental and physical well-being include setting boundaries, prioritising self-care, and giving rise to a healthy work-life balance. By addressing burnout, you safeguard your long-term productivity, creativity, and overall success in leading your startup.

Recognising Signs of Burnout

Entrepreneurship is a demanding journey that can take a toll on your mental and physical health. It is important to recognise the signs of burnout, such as feeling exhausted, overwhelmed, or disconnected from your work. By being aware of these signs, you can take proactive steps to prevent burnout before it takes a toll on your well-being.

Implementing Proactive Strategies

To prevent and overcome burnout, it is important to implement proactive strategies for maintaining your mental and physical well-being. This may include setting boundaries around your work, prioritising self-care activities such as exercise and meditation, and giving rise to a healthy work-life balance. By taking care of yourself, you can ensure that you have the energy and resilience needed to lead your startup effectively.

Safeguarding Long-term Success

Addressing burnout is not just important for your own well-being but also for the success of your startup. By prioritising your mental and physical health, you safeguard your long-term productivity, creativity, and overall success as a founder. Taking care of yourself allows you to bring your best self to your work, leading to better decision-making and, ultimately, a more successful startup.

Building a Support System

A robust founder support network is essential for providing encouragement, sharing experiences, and offering valuable insights throughout the entrepreneurial journey. It provides emotional, professional, and strategic support, fostering resilience, growth, and overall success in building and leading a startup.

Establishing a Support Network

Building a support system is essential for navigating the challenges of entrepreneurship. This network may include mentors, advisers, peers, and friends who offer diverse perspectives, guidance, and encouragement during challenging times. By surrounding yourself with supportive individuals, you can gain valuable insights, learn from the experiences of others, and stay motivated during difficult times.

Developing Collaboration and Support

A strong support system serves as a safety net during challenging times, providing a platform for exchanging ideas, seeking advice, and learning from the collective wisdom of peers. By developing a collaborative and supportive ecosystem, you can enhance your resilience, growth, and overall success in the startup journey. Whether you're facing a difficult decision or dealing with a setback, your support network can provide the guidance and encouragement you need to keep moving forward.

Investing in Personal and Professional Well-being

Establishing and nurturing a strong support system is an investment in your personal and professional well-being. By surrounding yourself with supportive individuals who believe in you and your vision, you can stay motivated, focused, and resilient in the face of challenges. Whether you're seeking advice on strategy, feedback on your ideas, or simply a listening ear, your support network is there to help you succeed.

Seeking Mentorship and Advice from Experienced Entrepreneurs

You would benefit immensely from seeking mentorship and advice from experienced entrepreneurs, as it provides a unique opportunity to learn from those who have navigated similar challenges. Mentorship offers valuable insights, accelerates learning, and provides a sounding board for critical decisions, enhancing your strategic capabilities.

Learning from Experience

Experienced entrepreneurs have invaluable insights and wisdom gained from years of experience. By seeking mentorship and advice from these individuals, you can accelerate your learning curve and avoid common pitfalls. Whether you're facing a specific challenge or seeking guidance on long-term strategy, a mentor can provide the perspective and advice you need to succeed.

Enhancing Strategic Capabilities

Mentorship provides a unique opportunity to enhance your strategic capabilities as a founder. By learning from someone who has been there before, you can gain a deeper understanding of the challenges and opportunities that lie ahead. Whether you're navigating a major pivot or planning for growth, a mentor can provide the guidance and support you need to make informed decisions and achieve your goals.

Developing Personal and Professional Growth

Cultivating a mentor-mentee relationship is beneficial not only for your startup but also for your personal and professional growth. A mentor can provide valuable feedback, challenge your assumptions, and help you develop the skills and mindset needed to succeed as a founder. By embracing mentorship, you can accelerate your growth, expand your network, and achieve your full potential as an entrepreneur.

Embracing Setbacks as Learning Opportunities

The startup journey is like adventuring in unknown territory, where there will be ups and downs, including hardships and setbacks. Embracing setbacks as learning opportunities is fundamental to the growth mindset of successful founders. Each setback presents a chance to iterate, adapt, and enhance strategies, contributing to the continuous improvement and resilience of the startup.

Viewing Setbacks as Stepping Stones

Setbacks are an inevitable part of the entrepreneurial journey. Rather than fearing them, successful founders embrace setbacks as opportunities for growth and learning. Each setback offers insights, revealing areas for improvement and innovation. By viewing setbacks as stepping stones to success, founders can develop a culture of innovation and encourage the team to approach challenges with a solution-oriented mindset.

Learning and Adapting

Each setback provides valuable learning experiences that can ultimately contribute to the long-term success of the startup. By embracing setbacks as learning opportunities, founders can iterate, adapt, and enhance their strategies, ultimately making their startups more resilient and successful. Rather than dwelling on failures, successful founders use setbacks as a catalyst for growth and innovation.

Developing a Culture of Resilience

Developing a culture that views setbacks as learning opportunities promotes resilience, adaptability, and a continuous drive for improvement within the startup team. By encouraging team members to embrace challenges and learn from failures, founders can create an environment where innovation thrives and success is inevitable. Ultimately, it is this culture of resilience that sets successful startups apart from the rest.

Developing Resilience to Bounce Back Stronger

Resilience is the ability to bounce back stronger from challenges, setbacks, and failures. Developing resilience involves cultivating a growth mindset, staying adaptable, and maintaining a positive perspective even in difficult situations. As a resilient founder, you inspire the same resilience in your team, creating a culture that thrives on challenges and sees them as opportunities for growth.

Cultivating a Growth Mindset

Resilience begins with a growth mindset – the belief that challenges and setbacks are opportunities for growth and learning. By cultivating a growth mindset, founders can maintain a positive perspective even in difficult situations, inspiring the same resilience in their team members. Rather than dwelling on failures, resilient founders focus on solutions and opportunities for improvement.

Staying Adaptable

In the fast-paced world of entrepreneurship, adaptability is key to success. Resilient founders are able to adapt to changing circumstances, pivot when necessary, and stay focused on their long-term goals. By staying adaptable, founders can navigate the inevitable ups and downs of the startup journey with grace and confidence, inspiring the same resilience in their team members.

Inspiring Resilience in Others

As a resilient founder, you have the power to inspire resilience in your team members. By leading by example, staying positive, and maintaining a solutions-oriented mindset, you can create a culture that thrives on challenges and sees setbacks as opportunities for growth. Ultimately, it is this culture of resilience that sets successful startups apart from the rest, enabling them to bounce back stronger from challenges and achieve their long-term goals.

FOUNDERS' INSPIRATION: SUSTAINING MOTIVATION AND FOCUS

As a founder, staying inspired is essential for maintaining motivation, focus, and resilience throughout the entrepreneurial journey. Here are some tips on finding inspiration and keeping it alive:

Finding Inspiration from Success Stories and Role Models

Drawing inspiration from success stories and role models provides you with a roadmap for your own journey. Learning from others' experiences helps you navigate challenges, make informed decisions, and envision the possibilities of success. By cultivating a mindset that seeks inspiration, you contribute to continuous learning, adaptability, and sustained motivation within your startup.

Staying Inspired with Continuous Learning

Continuous exposure to inspirational content, whether through books, talks, or networking, fuels creativity and drive within you as a founder. It is essential to continuously learn and stay updated on industry trends, emerging technologies, and market shifts. This commitment to continuous learning reflects a growth mindset, innovation, and strategic agility within you, your co-founders, and your startup team.

Approaching Challenges with Enthusiasm

Staying inspired contributes to a positive mindset, enabling you to approach challenges with enthusiasm and a solution-oriented approach. By keeping your inspiration alive, you maintain the drive and energy needed to overcome obstacles and achieve your startup's goals. Whether it is through success stories, role models, or continuous learning, finding inspiration is key to sustaining motivation and focus as a founder.

Balancing Work and Life: Prioritising Well-being for Long-term Success

Achieving a work-life balance is crucial for your overall well-being as a founder. You can prioritise personal well-being alongside professional commitments along the following lines:

Strategies for Achieving a Work-Life Balance

Achieving a work-life balance involves setting boundaries, prioritising tasks, and incorporating leisure and self-care activities into your daily routine. Establishing clear boundaries between work and personal life contributes to sustained energy, focus, and creativity during working hours. By prioritising personal well-being, you can navigate the demands of entrepreneurship with resilience and longevity.

Prioritising Personal Well-being Alongside Professional Commitments

Your well-being is paramount, requiring you to prioritise personal health, mental wellness, and relationships alongside your professional commitments. Recognising the interconnectedness of personal and professional aspects develops a holistic approach to success and longevity in the entrepreneurial journey. Prioritising well-being ensures that you can bring your best to the challenges and opportunities of building and leading a startup.

Enhancing Productivity and Preventing Burnout

A balanced approach enhances productivity, prevents burnout, and develops a healthy integration of personal and professional aspects of life. By prioritising self-care and personal well-being, you can sustain your energy, creativity, and long-term success as a founder. Whether it is through exercise, meditation, spending time with loved ones, or pursuing hobbies, taking care of yourself is essential for achieving a work-life balance and thriving in the fast-paced world of entrepreneurship.

Finding inspiration, staying motivated, and prioritising well-being is essential for your success and longevity as a founder. By cultivating a mindset that seeks inspiration, prioritising personal well-being, and achieving a work-life balance, you can sustain your energy, creativity, and resilience throughout the entrepreneurial journey.

LEARNING FROM SUCCESSFUL STARTUPS

In the dynamic landscape of entrepreneurship, new startups often find themselves navigating uncharted waters. However, they need not embark on their journey alone. Learning from the successes and failures of other thriving startups can serve as a beacon of guidance. By studying the strategies, innovations, and approaches of successful ventures, new startups gain valuable insights into market trends, customer preferences, and effective business models.

Whether it is about understanding how to cultivate a vibrant company culture, leveraging digital platforms for marketing, or optimising operational efficiency, the experiences of established startups offer invaluable lessons.

Embracing a culture of learning from peers gives rise to innovation, resilience, and adaptability, propelling emerging startups towards sustainable growth and success in the competitive business landscape.

As a new startup founder, it is crucial to learn from the experiences of other successful startups. One of the key lessons to take away is the importance of building a strong and capable team. When looking at other startups, it is essential to identify the key skills and expertise required to drive the startup's growth and success. This includes technical proficiency, industry knowledge, leadership experience, and a background in entrepreneurship.

By assembling a team with diverse skill sets, including technology development, product management, marketing, sales, finance, and operations, you can ensure that all aspects of the business are covered.

Analysing Success Stories from Various Sectors

Moreover, you should emphasise the relevant experience, accomplishments, and contributions of each team member to previous projects or ventures. Highlighting the track record of success and valuable experience of team members is essential for gaining the trust and confidence of investors. By showcasing the strengths of the team, you can demonstrate its readiness to tackle challenges and achieve success.

Extracting Lessons and Insights from Established Startups

Another important lesson to learn from successful startups is the value of cultivating a collaborative culture. Startups that promote open communication, creativity, and innovation within their teams are more likely to succeed. By creating a collaborative and inclusive team culture, you can ensure that your team members are motivated and engaged.

It is important to promote a shared vision and mission that aligns with your startup's goals and values. This will inspire team members to work towards common objectives and ensure that everyone is on the same page.

Providing opportunities for professional development, mentorship, and continuous learning is crucial for empowering team members and enabling their career growth. Investing in the development of the team will not only benefit individual team members but also the startup as a whole. By offering opportunities for growth and learning, you can attract top talent and retain your team members in the long run.

Understanding Their Journeys and Strategies

As a startup founder, you should learn from successful startups about the importance of resilience and adaptability. Navigating challenges and setbacks is an inevitable part of the startup journey. By demonstrating resilience, adaptability, and problem-solving skills, startup founders can show investors that they have what it takes to succeed.

Successful startups have shown examples of how they have overcome obstacles, pivoted in response to market feedback, and iterated on product development to achieve success. By highlighting these examples, startup founders can showcase their ability to thrive in dynamic and uncertain environments, embracing change as an opportunity for growth and improvement.

BUILDING AN EFFECTIVE FOUNDING TEAM

Forming the right founding team is critical for the success of any startup. A well-balanced team comprising individuals with complementary skills, expertise, and personalities can ensure conflict-free, speedy progress and long-term success.

One effective approach is to create a founding team consisting of a hustler, a geek, and a rainmaker, each bringing unique strengths and perspectives to the table.

Hustler

The hustler is the visionary, the driving force behind the startup, and the one who is adept at turning ideas into action. Their primary focus is on driving growth, building relationships, and acquiring customers. Key attributes of a hustler include:

Networking and Sales Skills

Hustlers are excellent networkers and have the ability to build and maintain relationships with customers, investors, and partners. They are skilled at selling the vision of the startup and convincing others to buy into it.

Marketing Expertise

Hustlers are responsible for creating and executing marketing strategies to promote the startup and its products or services. They have a deep understanding of customer needs and preferences and know how to position the startup effectively in the market.

Leadership Qualities

Hustlers are natural leaders who can inspire and motivate their teams to achieve their goals. They are ambitious, charismatic, and thrive in fast-paced environments.

Geek

The geek is the technical expert responsible for bringing the product or service to life. They are skilled in product development, technology, and engineering. Key attributes of a geek include:

Technical Expertise

Geeks have a deep understanding of technology and are proficient in coding, design, and problem-solving. They are responsible for building and refining the product or service to ensure it meets the needs of the market and exceeds customer expectations.

Innovative Thinking

Geeks are passionate about technology and innovation and are always looking for ways to improve and optimise. They are creative problem solvers who can think outside the box and come up with innovative solutions to complex problems.

Detail-Oriented

Geeks are highly analytical and detail-oriented, ensuring that every aspect of the product or service is carefully thought out and executed. They have a keen eye for detail and strive for perfection in everything they do.

Rainmaker

The rainmaker is the strategist responsible for bringing in the resources and opportunities needed for the startup to succeed. They are skilled in business development, fundraising, and strategic planning. Key attributes of a rainmaker include:

Business Development Skills

Rainmakers are responsible for building partnerships, securing funding, and identifying new market opportunities. They have a keen eye for spotting opportunities and are skilled at turning them into tangible results.

Fundraising Expertise

Rainmakers are adept at raising capital from investors and other sources. They have strong negotiation skills and know how to pitch the startup effectively to potential investors.

Strategic Thinking

Rainmakers are strategic thinkers who can see the big picture and develop plans to achieve the startup's long-term goals. They are creative problem solvers who can anticipate challenges and develop solutions to overcome them.

Other Key Attributes

Ensuring Conflict-Free, Speedy Progress

To ensure conflict-free, speedy progress, and long-term success, it is essential to establish clear roles and responsibilities for each member of the founding team. This helps to prevent misunderstandings and conflicts and ensures that everyone is aligned and working towards the same goals.

Clear Communication

Effective communication is key to the success of any team. Regular team meetings, brainstorming sessions, and check-ins can help keep everyone on the same page and ensure that progress is being made efficiently.

Shared Vision and Goals

It is important for the founding team to share a common vision and goals for the startup. By aligning on the startup's mission, values, and objectives, the team can work together more effectively towards a shared purpose.

Mutual Respect and Trust

Building a culture of mutual respect and trust is essential for a conflict-free work environment. Each member of the founding team should feel valued and respected for their contributions and trust each other to do their part in achieving the startup's goals.

By leveraging the diverse strengths and expertise of a well-balanced founding team, startups can navigate the challenges of the startup journey with confidence and achieve their goals more effectively. The combination of a hustler, a geek, and a rainmaker ensures that all aspects of the business are covered, setting the stage for success and growth.

STARTUP RECIPE

> Discover various important ingredients in raising a startup, its preparation recipe, and the life-and-death roadblock validations required along the entrepreneurial journey.
>
> It must be clearly noted and understood that until you are in sync with all the required characteristics of a startup founder, do not move to start executing your business plan. Also, note well that until you have a well-worked-out mission, co-founder team, minimum value proposition or product concept, business plan, and financial projections in place, do not spend any money on any technology development, operational expenditures, or human resources.

KEY STARTUP INGREDIENTS

Clear Vision and Mission

A clear vision and mission, which address real-world problem(s), provide the foundation for your startup, outlining long-term goals and the path to achieving them. This clarity serves as a guide for decision-making, aligning actions with the overarching purpose of the startup. Do not just come up with an idea; identify the real-world problem that your idea solves! Successful startups identify market problems and offer effective solutions. Addressing real issues faced by people contributes to the relevance and value of your startup in the market.

Build a Co-founder Team through Effective Leadership

Assemble a diverse and skilled co-founder team that collaborates effectively. Develop a culture where every team member's contribution enhances the overall success and innovation of the startup. Lead with confidence, inspiration, and clear direction. Effective leadership motivates the co-founder team and aligns everyone towards your common goal(s) as the leader.

Market Validation, Customer-Centric and Unique Value Proposition (UVP)

Thorough market validation and research ensure there is a genuine need for your product or service. Understanding the target market, customer needs, and competitors is essential for informed decision-making and strategic planning. Clearly communicate what makes your startup unique and why customers should choose your product or service.

A strong, Unique Value Proposition distinguishes your startup from competitors and attracts your target audience. Prioritise your customers by actively seeking feedback and understanding their needs. Make continuous improvements to your offerings based on customer insights. Develop a solid marketing strategy to promote your startup. Building a recognisable brand enhances visibility and distinguishes your startup in the market.

Strong Business Model with Strategic and Financial Planning

Develop a robust business model that outlines how your startup will generate revenue. Ensure the model is sustainable and adaptable to changes in the market as your business evolves. Create a detailed business plan with specific goals, including both short-term and long-term success criteria, adaptability to unforeseen challenges, and capitalising on opportunities. Manage finances wisely by budgeting effectively and forecasting future needs. Optimising resources ensures the sustainability and growth of your startup.

Adaptive, Agile, Persistent Mind and Communication Skills

Be ready to adapt and pivot to market shifts and changes. An agile mindset allows for iterative product development and flexibility to meet evolving customer needs. Clearly communicate your vision and goals to stakeholders.

Strong communication builds trust and develops positive relationships with investors, customers, and team members. Stay updated on industry trends and technological advancements. Adapt your strategies to remain relevant and capitalise on emerging opportunities. Develop resilience to step sideways or pivot from challenges.

Persistence, coupled with a positive attitude, ensures that setbacks are viewed as opportunities for growth and improvement through analysis and pivoting. In the following chapters, these points are explained in detail.

Networking and Partnerships

Partnerships offer valuable opportunities for growth, collaboration, and shared success. Building relationships in your industry through networking can lead to significant risk mitigation. For example, a partnership with a strategic supplier offering equity in return for a long-term supply contract, where costs are traded with paid-up equity, is an indirect way to raise funds and cover future supplier costs.

Procurement partnerships can be combined with partnerships with customer channel partners, which can secure base revenues essential for a startup. A channel partner that can deliver key customers is invaluable for angel investors to feel confident in investing in startups at the beginning of their journey.

Compliance and Legal Understanding

Understand and comply with legal requirements to protect your business. Adhering to rules and regulations helps avoid potential legal issues that could impact your startup. Additionally, in certain industries, compliance with regulations is a prerequisite to delivering products or services to customers. For example, regulatory approvals are a prerequisite for a financial services company with the RBI (Reserve Bank of India) to deliver products and services to end users.

SLIPPERY ROAD AHEAD - CAUTION

It is important to appreciate the pitfalls that founders can face at the very initial stages of their startup and where and when they need to be careful and mindful. The first and most important stage is selecting the right co-founder team members with complementary skills and domain knowledge.

Before you embark on the exciting journey of starting your own venture as the lead founder, I want to offer a word of caution drawn from the collective wisdom of those who have navigated the unpredictable terrain of startups. These nuggets of advice can serve as invaluable guideposts as you set forth on this thrilling adventure.

Co-Founders Teaming – Complementary Skills and Gelling

The significance of your choice of co-founders is THE most important decision. This is not just a business partnership; it is a shared commitment, a mutual understanding of the vision, and a journey laden with challenges. Ensure that your co-founder aligns not only with your professional aspirations but also with your values and work ethic. This alliance is the bedrock of your startup, so choose wisely and build a partnership founded on trust and shared goals.

The strength of a co-founding team lies not just in individual brilliance but in the seamless synergy of complementary skills. A good founder team should have a hustler (sales), a techie, and a finance expert. Look for co-founders who bring such expertise to the table—skills that fill the gaps in your own proficiency.

If one excels in technical aspects, consider a co-founder with strong business development skills. If you are adept at product ideation, a co-founder with a flair for marketing can complete the puzzle. This diversity of skills develops a well-rounded team, enabling you to tackle multifaceted challenges and capitalise on a broader range of opportunities.

Beyond skills, the temperament of your co-founders plays a pivotal role in the cohesion and resilience of your startup team. Startup life is inherently stressful and unpredictable, requiring a team that can navigate both successes and setbacks with grace. Seek co-founders whose temperaments align with the dynamic nature of entrepreneurship—individuals who are resilient, adaptable, and can maintain composure under pressure.

A harmonious blend of personalities contributes to a positive team culture and strengthens your collective ability to weather the storms that invariably come with the startup territory.

Impulsive Formation is Mostly Short-Lived

The impulse to form a startup quickly, particularly in the face of a compelling idea, is understandable. However, it is crucial to recognise that impulsive formations often lack the depth and compatibility needed for sustained success.

Take the time to thoroughly vet potential co-founders, ensuring alignment not only in goals but also in values and work ethics. Establishing a foundation built on mutual understanding and trust may take time, but it significantly enhances the longevity and effectiveness of your startup co-founders' team.

The selection of co-founders is akin to crafting a finely tuned ensemble where each instrument contributes uniquely to the symphony. Complementary skills, aligned temperaments, and a well-considered formation process are the cornerstones of a co-founding team that can navigate the complexities of startup life and stand the test of time. As you assemble your team, the harmony of skills and personalities should fortify your startup against the challenges ahead and propel it toward enduring success.

Transition from Employee to Startup Co-Founder

Transitioning from a stable job to the unpredictable world of startup entrepreneurship requires a profound shift in mindset. While the routine of a job offers a sense of security, the startup environment is characterised by constant change, uncertainty, and a high-level of risk.

As a co-founder, one must be prepared for the rollercoaster ride of ups and downs that come with building something from the ground up. This shift demands resilience, adaptability, and an unwavering belief in one's co-founder team vision.

Unlike a job, where tasks and responsibilities are often clearly defined, startup founders must navigate ambiguity and make decisions in the face of uncertainty. They need to be comfortable with the idea of wearing multiple hats, juggling various roles, and making tough decisions under pressure. Moreover, they must embrace failure as an inevitable part of the journey, seeing it not as a setback but as an opportunity to learn and grow.

Finally, this transition requires a fundamental change in mindset, from being a follower to becoming a leader, from seeking stability to embracing risk, and from conforming to established norms to challenging the status quo.

Infatuation

Raising a startup is in vogue, and it is cool to be known as a startup founder. One may be tempted to start a business like a friend who became a celebrity. It is almost like the glamour of acting in films or modelling, in which people are pulled in by infatuation. Passion is the driving force behind every startup, but be wary if infatuation is pulling you into it.

You also have to make a fair judgement about yourself—whether you have the attitude, resilience, and conviction critically required to raise your startup.

No 'Plan B'

While unwavering determination is an asset, it is equally important to acknowledge the need for contingency planning. Adopting a "no plan B" mindset might sound bold, but it is essential to recognise that unforeseen challenges are an inherent part of the entrepreneurial journey. Embrace courage, stay agile in your approach, and be firm in doing anything and everything to make your startup successful.

Plan B is like this—if your startup does not work out well in one year, then you will take up a job or join your family business. In such a case, this initiative is surely going to nose-dive. You have to go all-in, with all your strength and resources, with no option but to make your startup successful as if it is a matter of your survival.

Startup is a Business

The excitement of creating something new can be intoxicating. It is essential to remember that a startup, at its essence, is a business. This means that however passionate, tech-savvy, or innovative you may be, you must have a solid understanding of the fundamentals of running a business. Familiarise yourself with financial management, marketing strategies, customer acquisition, and operational intricacies. You have to remember only one fact—in the shortest time, your startup has to be profitable.

Know Your Subject Matter

Before you dive headfirst into the startup world, become a subject matter expert in your field. Know your industry, your market, and your potential competitors inside out. A profound understanding of your subject matter is not just a prerequisite; it is your armour against unforeseen challenges. Keep yourself informed, stay abreast of industry trends, and be ready to adapt your strategy as the landscape evolves.

Choose Your Startup Domain Carefully

The domain in which you choose to launch your startup is a pivotal decision that can significantly impact your journey. Carefully assess your strengths, interests, and market trends before settling on your startup's focus. Choosing a domain that aligns with your expertise and passion enhances your chances of success. Additionally, consider the market demand, competition, and potential for growth within your chosen domain. A thoughtful selection at this stage can set the stage for a more seamless and successful entrepreneurial voyage.

In essence, while the allure of entrepreneurship often centres around innovation and creativity, grounding your aspirations in a solid understanding of business principles and carefully selecting your startup domain can be the bedrock for sustained success.

As you embark on this dynamic adventure, may your decisions be informed, your passion unwavering, and your journey marked by the fruitful fusion of visionary ideas and practical business acumen.

STAGES IN A STARTUP LIFECYCLE

The startup lifecycle outlines the various stages a startup typically goes through from its inception to either successful maturity or premature closure. Each stage presents unique challenges, opportunities, and objectives.

Idea Generation - Pre-project Stage

The startup journey often begins with an idea—a solution to a problem or an opportunity perceived by the founders. During this stage, founders engage in activities such as brainstorming, conducting market research, identifying pain points, validating the idea's feasibility, and assessing market demand. The goal is to refine the initial idea into a viable business concept that addresses a significant need in the market.

Validation and Prototyping – Design Stage

In this stage, the startup seeks to validate its business idea and build a prototype MVP to test the concept. Activities include conducting extensive customer interviews, creating a prototype MVP, gathering feedback, and iterating based on user responses. The aim is to validate assumptions, understand customer needs, and refine the product or service to achieve product-market fit.

Growth and Scaling - Rollout Acceptance Stage

At this stage, the startup aims to scale its operations, grow its customer base, and increase revenue. Activities include scaling marketing efforts, expanding the team, optimising operations, improving customer retention, and seeking additional funding if needed. The objective is to achieve sustainable growth, expand market reach, and solidify the startup's position in the industry.

Launch and Early Traction - Development and Test Stage

With a validated product or service, the startup officially launches and focuses on acquiring initial customers. Activities during this stage include marketing and promotion, implementing customer acquisition strategies, refining the product based on early feedback, and establishing a strong brand presence. The goal is to gain early traction, acquire initial customers, and generate revenue to validate the business model.

Maturity and Expansion – Adopt Stage

Having established itself in the market, the startup seeks to expand its offerings, enter new markets, or diversify its product/service portfolio. Activities may include launching new products or features, expanding into new geographical regions or customer segments, forming strategic partnerships, and exploring potential acquisitions. The goal is to maintain growth momentum, capture a larger market share, and solidify the startup's position as a market leader.

Exit or Sustainability – Close Stage

At this stage, the startup may choose to exit through various means, such as acquisition, Initial Public Offering (IPO), or continue operating as a sustainable business. Activities include evaluating exit opportunities, negotiating deals with potential acquirers or investors, or focusing on long-term sustainability and profitability. The goal is to maximise returns for stakeholders, whether through an exit event or sustainable long-term growth.

Key Considerations

Progression through these stages is not always linear, and startups may iterate or revisit previous stages as they evolve. Startups require various resources, including funding, talent, and mentorship, at each stage to navigate challenges and capitalise on opportunities. Successful startups demonstrate agility and adaptability, responding to market feedback and evolving trends to stay competitive and relevant in their industries.

SIX PHASES OF GROWTH IN A STARTUP LIFECYCLE

The lifecycle of a startup can be broadly divided into several distinct phases, each with its own set of challenges, goals, and objectives.

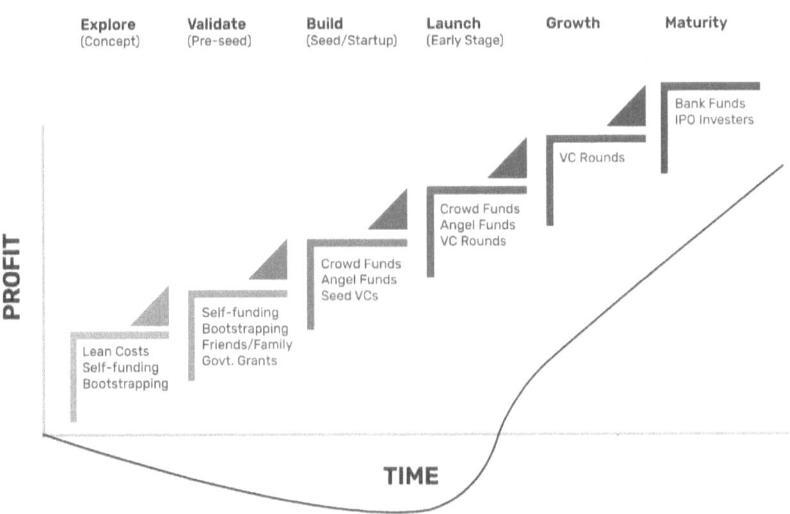

Explore

In the exploration phase, entrepreneurs embark on the journey of identifying and exploring potential business ideas. This involves brainstorming, conducting thorough research on market trends, and assessing various opportunities.

Ideation

During ideation, entrepreneurs engage in the process of generating and refining business ideas. This often involves intensive brainstorming sessions, market research, and identifying pain points or unmet needs within the market. They explore different concepts, looking for innovative solutions that could potentially address significant market demands or solve existing problems.

Market Research

Market research plays a crucial role in this phase. Entrepreneurs conduct extensive analysis of market trends, customer needs, and the competitive landscape. They delve deep into understanding customer behaviour, preferences, and emerging trends to inform their business ideas. Through comprehensive market research, they identify opportunities and gaps within the market that their startup could potentially address.

Validation

Validation is another critical aspect of the exploration phase. Startups test the feasibility and viability of their ideas through preliminary research, surveys, and interviews with potential customers. The goal is to validate whether there is indeed a market demand for the proposed solution. This involves gathering feedback and insights from target customers to ensure that the business idea resonates with the intended market.

Validate

In the validation phase, startups seek to validate their business ideas and assumptions by gathering feedback from their target customers. This phase is crucial for determining whether there is indeed a market demand for the proposed solution.

MVP

The first step in this phase is MVP development. Startups begin by building an MVP with basic features. The MVP is designed to test core assumptions and gather feedback from early adopters and target customers. It allows startups to validate their product concept with minimal investment and risk.

Customer Validation

Customer validation is another essential aspect of this phase. Startups engage with early adopters and target customers to validate product-market fit and gather feedback on the MVP. This feedback is invaluable for iterating and refining the product or business model. By listening to their customers and incorporating their feedback, startups can ensure that they are building a product that meets the needs of their target market.

The validation phase also involves iteration. Startups continuously iterate and refine their product or business model based on customer feedback and market validation. This iterative process is fundamental to the evolution and success of the startup. By iterating quickly and responding to customer feedback, startups can increase their chances of success and build a product that truly resonates with their target market.

Build

Once the business idea is validated, startups transition into the build phase, where they focus on developing the product or service in preparation for launch.

Product Development

During the build phase, startups focus on product development. They build the full-featured product or service based on the validated MVP, incorporating additional features and functionalities to meet the needs of their target market. Product development is a collaborative process that involves designers, developers, and other key team members working together to bring the product to life.

In addition to product development, startups also focus on building the necessary technical infrastructure to support the product or service. This may involve setting up servers, databases, and software tools to ensure that the product can scale and meet the needs of its users.

Team Building

Team building is another critical aspect of the build phase. Startups hire key team members, such as developers, designers, and marketers, to support product development and overall business operations. Building the right team is essential for the success of the startup, as it ensures that they have the skills and expertise needed to bring their vision to life.

Launch

The launch phase marks the official introduction of the product or service to the market. Startups aim to generate buzz, attract initial users, and acquire early customers.

Marketing Campaigns

During the launch phase, startups focus on marketing campaigns. They plan and execute marketing campaigns to create awareness and generate excitement around the product launch. This may involve social media marketing, email marketing, influencer partnerships, and other marketing tactics to reach their target audience.

Customer / User Acquisition

Customer/user acquisition is another key aspect of the launch phase. Startups focus on acquiring early adopters and customers through various channels, such as social media, email marketing, and partnerships. By acquiring early customers, startups can generate momentum and traction in the market, which is essential for the success of the product or service.

PR Outreach

In addition to marketing campaigns and user acquisition, startups also focus on PR outreach during the launch phase. They engage with press and media outlets to secure coverage and publicity for the product launch. This helps to build brand visibility and credibility, which is essential for gaining the trust of potential customers and investors.

Growth

In the growth phase, startups focus on scaling their operations, acquiring more customers, and expanding their market reach.

Scaling Operations

One of the key activities during the growth phase is scaling operations. Startups scale up production, distribution, and customer support to meet the growing demand for their product or service. This may involve expanding their team, investing in new technology and infrastructure, and optimising their processes to improve efficiency and scalability.

Customer Acquisition

Customer acquisition is another critical aspect of the growth phase. Startups scale their marketing efforts and optimise customer acquisition channels to attract a larger user base. This may involve investing in paid advertising, expanding into new markets, and leveraging partnerships to reach new customers.

Monetisation

Monetisation is also an essential consideration during the growth phase. Startups implement monetisation strategies, such as subscription plans, advertising, or freemium models, to generate revenue and sustain growth. By monetising their product or service, startups can reinvest revenue into further growth and expansion, ensuring the long-term success of the business.

Maturity

The maturity phase is reached when the startup has achieved stability and sustainability in its operations. It is characterised by steady growth, a mature customer base, and an established market presence.

Diversification

During the maturity phase, startups focus on diversification. They may expand into new markets, products, or services to diversify their revenue streams and mitigate risks. By diversifying their offerings, startups can capitalise on new opportunities and ensure the long-term success of the business.

Optimisation

Optimisation is another key aspect of the maturity phase. Startups continuously optimise their business processes, products, and services to improve efficiency and profitability. This may involve streamlining operations, reducing costs, and improving the quality of their products and services to better meet the needs of their customers.

Long-term Planning

Long-term planning is also essential during the maturity phase. Startups develop long-term strategies and goals to sustain growth and maintain competitiveness in the market. This may involve expanding into new markets, investing in research and development, and staying ahead of emerging trends to ensure the continued success of the business.

Throughout the startup life cycle, founders face various challenges and uncertainties, but each phase presents opportunities for learning, growth, and innovation. By navigating these phases effectively, startups can increase their chances of success and achieve their goals.

STARTING POINT

In this chapter the starting point for your startup is elaborated. Starting from an idea and how it is required to be explored further is an important process, required to be clearly understood before getting to the further detailing and execution.

Use of tools for detailing, defining customer persona is a critical exercise which will define the focus of your startup. Based on the primary understanding, detailing of the customer value proposition and developing a business plan is given in this chapter. You will also learn about the formation of your company and the statutory compliances required.

The foundation of a successful startup lies in a well-conceived idea that addresses a genuine market need. Ideation is not merely about brainstorming; it is about identifying problems worth solving and creating solutions that resonate with the target audience. Market research becomes a crucial companion in this journey, providing the necessary validation and insights.

IDEATION AND MARKET RESEARCH

In this chapter, we dive into the intricacies of ideation, exploring techniques to generate innovative ideas and validate their feasibility. Market research takes centre stage, guiding founders on how to analyse market trends, understand customer behaviours, and assess competition. By the end of this chapter, aspiring entrepreneurs will have a robust framework to shape their startup ideas, ensuring their relevance and potential for success in the Indian market.

Generating and Validating Startup Ideas

Start by brainstorming potential business ideas, considering your interests, expertise, and market needs. Validate these ideas through market research, surveys, and feedback from potential customers to ensure they meet a real demand.

Conducting Market Research in the Indian Context

Dive into the specifics of the Indian market, understanding cultural nuances, economic trends, and consumer behaviours. Analyse competitors, regulatory environments, and potential obstacles to tailor your business strategy effectively.

Identifying Target Audience and Market Trends

Define your target audience precisely, considering demographics, psychographics, and behaviours. Stay abreast of market trends to align your product or service offerings with evolving consumer preferences and industry advancements. For the complete guide, consider seeking additional resources or consulting with experts who can provide tailored advice based on your specific industry and startup goals.

PREPARATIONS AND GROUND WORK

Create a Business Model Canvas

Creating a Business Model Canvas (BMC) is a visual framework that helps entrepreneurs and business owners describe, design, challenge, invent, and pivot their business models. The BMC was introduced by Alexander Osterwalder and Yves Pigneur in their book "Business Model Generation."

The Business Model Canvas (BMC) is a valuable tool for several reasons: offering a structured and visual way for entrepreneurs and businesses to articulate, design, and understand key aspects of their business model. Here is why it is important and helpful:

Clarity and Alignment

The BMC provides a clear and concise overview of all the critical components of a business in one single view. This helps align team members and stakeholders on the same page regarding the business model, developing a shared understanding.

Visualisation of Business Model

It offers a visual representation, making it easier for individuals to comprehend complex business models. This visual aspect aids in quickly communicating the essence of the business to others.

Iterative and Dynamic

The canvas is designed to be a dynamic tool that can be easily updated and modified. This is crucial for businesses that need to adapt and iterate their models in response to changes in the market, customer feedback, or internal factors.

Holistic View

By breaking down the business into key building blocks, the BMC encourages a holistic perspective. Entrepreneurs can see how each component interacts with others, promoting a more comprehensive understanding of their business model.

Identification of Opportunities and Risks

It helps in identifying potential gaps, opportunities, and risks in the business model. By examining each building block, businesses can uncover areas for improvement or innovation.

Communication Tool

The visual nature of the canvas makes it an effective communication tool, especially when interacting with stakeholders, investors, or team members who may not be familiar with the intricate details of the business model.

Strategic Decision-Making

The BMC assists in strategic decision-making by providing a framework for evaluating different aspects of the business simultaneously. This can be particularly useful when considering changes or expansions in the business.

Resource Optimisation

It helps in identifying and optimising the use of resources. By understanding key resources and activities, businesses can allocate resources more efficiently to support their value proposition and overall strategy.

Startup Planning and Validation

For startups, the BMC is a valuable tool for planning and validating their business model before committing significant resources. It allows entrepreneurs to test hypotheses and make adjustments based on market feedback.

Facilitates Collaboration

The canvas is often used in collaborative settings, where team members can contribute their insights and perspectives. This collaborative approach fosters engagement and can lead to a more well-rounded understanding of the business model.

The Business Model Canvas is important and helpful because it provides a structured and visual way to understand, communicate, and iterate on a business model. It is a versatile tool that can be applied across various industries and stages of a business, from startups to established enterprises.

Step-by-step Guide on How to Create a Business Model Canvas

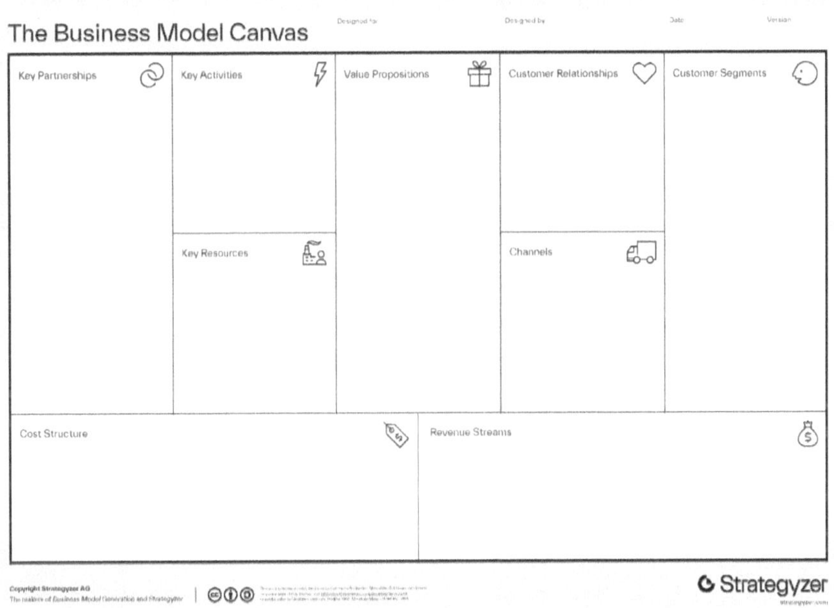

Start with a Blank Canvas

Draw a large canvas on a whiteboard paper, or use a digital tool or go to https://shorturl.at/rGc4z or download from

The canvas is typically divided into 9 key building blocks.

Identify Customer Segments

Define the different groups of people or organisations that your business aims to serve. These are your customers.

Value Propositions

Clearly articulate the unique value your product or service provides to each customer segment. This is what sets your business apart.

Channels

Determine the various ways you will reach and deliver value to your customers. This includes distribution channels, sales channels, and communication channels.

Customer Relationships

Describe the type of relationship you intend to establish with each customer segment. This could be personal assistance, self-service, automated services, etc.

Revenue Streams

Identify how your business will generate revenue from each customer segment. This may include one-time sales, subscription models, licensing, etc.

Key Resources

List the essential assets and resources required to deliver your value proposition, reach customers, maintain relationships, and earn revenue.

Key Activities

Outline the key activities your business must perform to deliver its value proposition, reach customers, and maintain operations.

Key Partnerships

Identify external entities (suppliers, partners, etc.) that your business will collaborate with to enhance its value proposition or optimise its operations.

Cost Structure

Detail the costs associated with operating your business. This includes fixed and variable costs, as well as economies of scale.

Fill in the Canvas

Go through each building block and fill in the details. Use concise and clear language. You can use post-it notes or digital tools for easy modification and sharing.

Review and Iterate

Once the canvas is filled, step back and review the overall picture. Consider how each building block relates to the others. Discuss and iterate based on feedback and insights.

Update as Needed

The Business Model Canvas is a dynamic tool. Update it as your business evolves, especially when you experience changes in the market, industry, or internal operations.

The Business Model Canvas is a flexible tool, and there is no one-size-fits-all approach. It is meant to be adapted to your specific business context and can be revisited and revised as your business grows and changes.

Specify Key Resources

Identify the critical assets and resources your business needs to operate. This includes physical, intellectual, human, and financial resources. Ensure your resources align with your key activities and value proposition.

List Key Activities

Identify the key tasks and activities necessary to deliver your value proposition. Consider production, problem-solving, platform development, and customer support. Ensure your activities support your revenue model and customer relationships.

CUSTOMER PERSONA

Understanding Customer Personas and How to Create Them

A customer persona, also known as a buyer persona, is a semi-fictional representation of an ideal customer based on market research and real data about your existing customers. It helps businesses understand their customers' needs, preferences, behaviours, and challenges, allowing for more targeted and effective marketing strategies.

Customer personas are essential tools for startups as they help align product development, marketing, and sales strategies with the specific needs and desires of target customers. By creating detailed personas, startups can tailor their messaging, improve customer engagement, and ultimately drive growth.

Importance of Customer Personas

1. Targeted Marketing and Messaging

   Customer personas allow startups to tailor their marketing messages to resonate with specific audience segments, leading to more effective communication and higher conversion rates.

2. Product Development

   Understanding the needs and pain points of different personas helps in designing and developing products or services that meet their specific requirements, increasing customer satisfaction and loyalty.

3. Improved Customer Experience

   By understanding the behaviours and preferences of your target customers, you can create a more personalised and satisfying customer experience.

4. Efficient Resource Allocation

   Personas help prioritise marketing efforts and budgets by focusing on the most valuable customer segments.

Creating a Customer Persona

Conduct Thorough Research

Gather Data:

Customer Interviews and Surveys: Talk directly to customers to gather insights about their needs, preferences, challenges, and decision-making processes.

Sales and Customer Service Teams: Leverage insights from team members who interact directly with customers.

Analytics and CRM Data: Analyse data from your website, social media, and CRM system to understand customer behaviour and demographics.

Competitor Analysis: Study competitors to identify common customer traits and market gaps.

Identify Key Demographics

Collect and analyse demographic information, including:

Age

Gender

Location

Education Level

Occupation

Income Level

Marital Status

This information helps in understanding who your customers are and their socio-economic background.

Understand Psychographics

Beyond demographics, delve into psychographics to understand the psychological attributes of your customers:

- Values and Beliefs: What do they care about? What drives their decisions?

- Interests and Hobbies: What do they enjoy doing in their free time?

- Lifestyle Choices: How do they spend their time and money?

- Challenges and Pain Points: What problems are they trying to solve?

- Goals and Motivations: What are their personal or professional goals?

Behavioural Insights

Analyse customer behaviours, such as:

- Buying Habits: What triggers a purchase? What are the buying patterns?

- Brand Interactions: How do they interact with your brand across different channels?

- Technology Usage: What devices and platforms do they use?

Create Persona Profiles

Based on the gathered data, create detailed persona profiles. Each persona should include:

- Persona Name: Give your persona a name for easy reference.

- Demographic Information: Summarise key demographic data.

- Background: Include a brief description of the persona's background, including education, career, and family life.

- Goals and Objectives: Outline what the persona aims to achieve, both personally and professionally.

- Challenges and Pain Points: List the primary challenges and pain points the persona faces.

- Behavioural Characteristics: Describe their buying habits, preferred communication channels, and any other relevant behaviours.

- Values and Motivations: Detail what motivates the persona and their core values.

Visual Representation

To make the personas more relatable and memorable, consider including visual elements such as:

- Photograph or Illustration: A generic image representing the persona.

- Quote: A hypothetical quote that captures the persona's outlook or common concerns.

Validate and Refine

After creating initial personas, validate them with real customer feedback. This process may involve:

- Testing Messaging: Test different messages and observe responses.

- Gathering Feedback: Regularly update personas based on new data and feedback.

Utilise Personas Across the Business

Ensure that all departments within your startup use the personas to guide decision-making. This includes:

- Marketing and Advertising: Tailoring campaigns and content to address the needs and interests of specific personas.

- Product Development: Designing features and solutions that meet the personas' needs.

- Sales and Customer Service: Training teams to understand and communicate effectively with different personas.

Creating customer personas is a strategic exercise that provides a deeper understanding of your target audience. By investing time in developing accurate and detailed personas, startups can create more personalised and effective marketing strategies, improve product development, and ultimately foster stronger relationships with their customers. Remember that personas are living documents; they should evolve as you gain more insights and as market conditions change.

CREATE A CRISP - CUSTOMER VALUE PROPOSITION

Having understood the Customer Persona, it is important to create the Customer Value Proposition (CVP).

CVP is critically important for several reasons, as it serves as the foundation for your marketing and business strategy.

Many important reasons for CVP being so crucial.

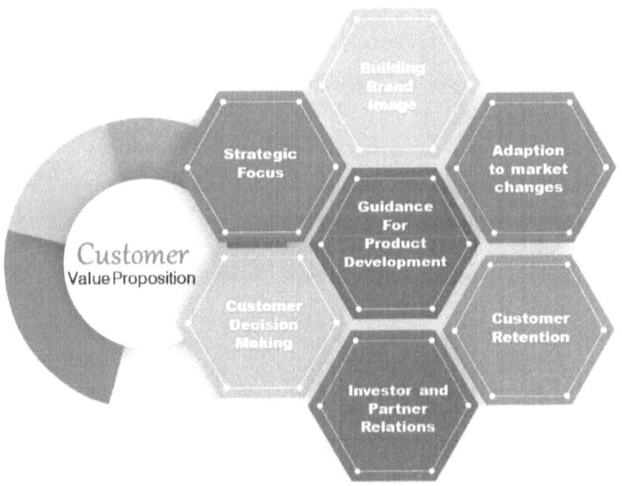

Differentiation and Competitive Advantage

A well-crafted CVP helps distinguish your product or service from competitors. It highlights what makes your offering unique, giving you a competitive advantage in the market.

Clear Communication of Value

It succinctly communicates the value your product or service delivers to customers. This clarity is essential in capturing the attention and interest of potential customers, helping them understand how your offering meets their needs.

Customer Understanding

Developing a CVP requires a deep understanding of your target audience. This process helps you identify their pain points, preferences, and priorities, allowing you to tailor your messaging to resonate with them effectively.

Effective Marketing and Sales

A compelling CVP forms the basis for your marketing and sales efforts. It provides a central message that can be used across various channels, making your marketing communications more consistent and impactful.

Customer Decision-Making

When customers are evaluating options in the market, a strong CVP can influence their decision-making process. It helps them see the benefits and value of your product, making it more likely they will choose your offering over alternatives.

Customer Retention

A clear and appealing value proposition not only attracts new customers but also contributes to customer retention. When customers consistently experience the promised value, they are more likely to remain loyal to your brand.

Guidance for Product Development

The process of defining a CVP often involves identifying key customer needs and preferences. This information is valuable for guiding product development and ensuring that your offerings align with customer expectations.

Strategic Focus

A strong CVP helps your team stay focused on the core value your business provides. It serves as a guiding principle for decision-making, ensuring that all aspects of your business strategy align with delivering that value to customers.

Building Brand Image

The CVP contributes to shaping your brand image. When consistently communicated and delivered, it establishes a positive perception of your brand in the minds of customers.

Investor and Partner Relations

A compelling CVP is essential when seeking investment or forming partnerships. Investors and partners want to understand the unique value your business brings to the market and why it is likely to succeed.

Adaptation to Market Changes

As markets evolve, a well-defined CVP allows your business to adapt to changes. Whether it is introducing new features or entering new markets, the core value proposition remains the anchor that guides strategic decisions.

Step-by-step Guide on How to Create a Crisp Customer Value Proposition

Understand Your Customer

Identify and understand your target customers. What are their pain points, needs, and desires? The more you know about your customers, the better you can tailor your value proposition to resonate with them.

Identify the Problem You Solve

Clearly articulate the problem or challenge your product or service solves. Your CVP should address a specific pain point or provide a solution to a problem that your target audience faces.

Highlight Key Benefits

Outline the key benefits your product or service brings to customers. Focus on the positive outcomes and improvements that users can expect. Consider both functional and emotional benefits.

Be Clear and Concise

Keep your CVP clear, concise, and easily understandable. Avoid jargon and technical language that may confuse your audience. Use simple and straightforward language that resonates with your target customers.

Differentiate Your Offering

Clearly communicate what sets your product apart from the competition. Highlight unique features, technology, or approaches that make your solution distinct and superior.

Emphasise Value, Not Just Features

Instead of just listing product features, emphasise the value those features bring to customers. Explain how your product addresses specific needs and adds value to their lives or businesses.

Quantify Where Possible

Whenever applicable, use numbers and data to quantify the benefits of your product. Whether it is cost savings, time efficiency, or performance improvements, providing concrete metrics adds credibility to your CVP.

Use Customer Language

Speak the language of your customers. Use terms and phrases that resonate with them. This creates a connection and makes your value proposition more relatable.

Address Objections

Anticipate potential objections or concerns your customers might have and proactively address them in your CVP. This builds trust and shows that you understand and care about your customers' needs.

Test and Iterate

Test your value proposition with a small group of target customers and gather feedback. Use the insights to refine and iterate on your messaging. A/B testing can be valuable in understanding what resonates best.

Create a Memorable Tagline

Develop a memorable and concise tagline that encapsulates your value proposition. This tagline should be easy to remember and effectively communicate the essence of your offering.

Visual Representation

Consider using visuals, such as infographics or videos, to enhance your CVP. Visuals can help convey complex ideas in a digestible format and make your value proposition more engaging.

Align with Brand Identity

Ensure that your CVP aligns with your overall brand identity. Consistency in messaging and branding builds a cohesive and recognisable image for your startup.

Continuously Refine

Your CVP is not static. As your business evolves and you learn more about your customers, continuously refine and update your value proposition to stay relevant and competitive.

A compelling Customer Value Proposition is a cornerstone of your overall marketing strategy. It should grab attention, resonate with your target audience, and convince them that your product or service is the solution they have been looking for.

The Customer Value Proposition is a fundamental element that influences how your business is perceived and how effectively it can attract and retain customers. It serves as the cornerstone for marketing, sales, and overall business strategy, playing a pivotal role in the success of your startup or business.

BUILDING A STRONG AND COMPELLING BUSINESS PLAN

Crafting a Comprehensive Business Plan

Once you have a certain level of clarity and conviction about your startup idea and have done the research, I strongly recommend to develop a detailed business plan for your startup, as the first step well before you do anything else or spend money. So much as it sounds academic, it is the most important part of your journey.

Develop a detailed business plan outlining your mission, vision, and strategic goals. Clearly articulate your value proposition, target market, and competitive advantage to attract stakeholders and guide your business's trajectory.

Creating a detailed business plan for startups is a crucial step in setting a clear direction for your startup and ensuring you have thought through all aspects of your business. Here is a comprehensive guide to help you structure your startup business plan

Executive Summary

- Briefly introduce your business concept, mission, and vision.

- Highlight your unique selling proposition (USP).
- Provide a snapshot of your financial projections.

Market Analysis

- Define your target market and customer segments.
- Conduct a thorough analysis of the industry and market trends.
- Identify your competitors and analyse their strengths and weaknesses.
- Highlight your competitive advantage.

Product or Service Line

- Describe your product or service in detail.
- Define your typical customer persona.
- Highlight its features, benefits, and how it addresses customer needs.
- Discuss any proprietary technology or intellectual property.

Marketing and Sales Strategy

- Outline your marketing and sales approach.
- Define your pricing strategy.
- Detail your sales channels and distribution methods.
- Develop a plan for customer acquisition and retention.

Financial Projections and Budgeting

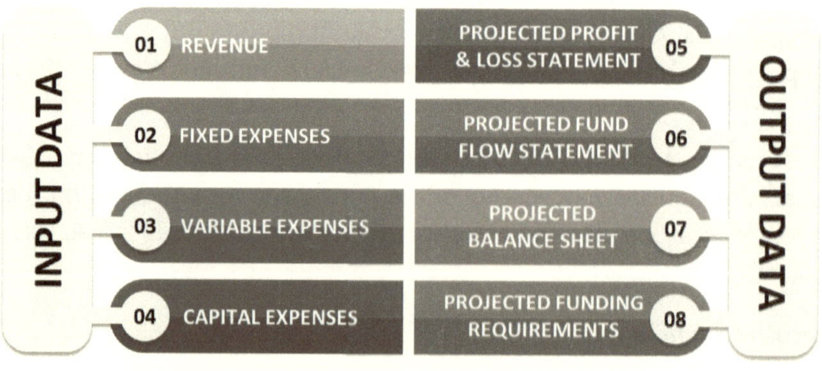

Create realistic financial projections and budgets to guide your financial decisions. Understand your startup costs, revenue streams, and cash flow requirements to ensure financial stability and growth.

Creating detailed financial projections for a startup is a crucial aspect of your business plan. It requires a careful analysis of your revenue streams, expenses, and financial assumptions. Here is a step-by-step guide to help you make comprehensive financial projections. Microsoft Excel is an excellent tool to create a detailed spreadsheet.

Choose a Revenue Model

- Decide how your business will make money.
- Common revenue models include sales, subscriptions, licensing, advertising, and freemium.
- Consider multiple revenue streams, if applicable.

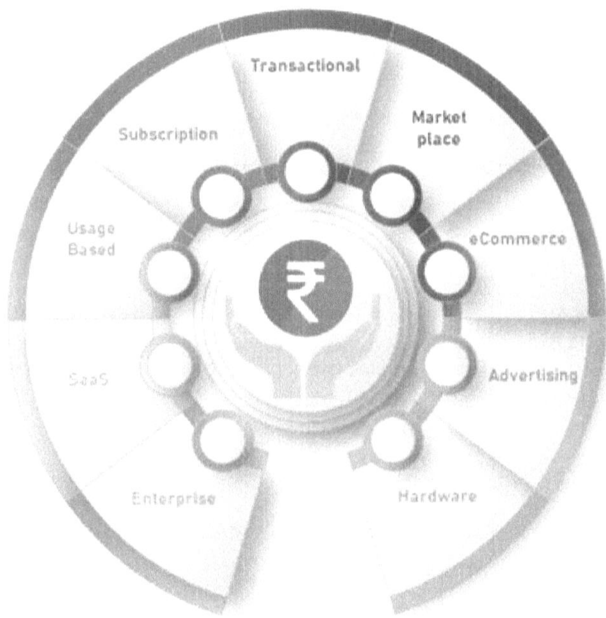

Revenue Forecast

- Start with a realistic estimate of your sales. Break it down by product or service.
- Consider market research, customer feedback, and industry trends.
- Project monthly or quarterly sales for the next 3 years.

Cost of Goods Sold (COGS)

- Determine the direct costs associated with producing your product or delivering your service.
- Include costs such as raw materials and manufacturing overhead.
- Calculate the gross profit by subtracting COGS from sales.

Operating Expenses

- List all fixed and variable operating expenses, including rent, utilities, salaries, marketing, and administrative costs.
- Differentiate between one-time startup costs and ongoing operational expenses.
- Group expenses by category for clarity.

Personnel Plan

- Provide details about your team, their roles, and their corresponding salaries.
- Include benefits, bonuses, and any other compensation-related costs.
- Consider future hiring plans as your business grows.

Cash Flow Projection

- Develop a detailed cash flow projection that includes both inflows and outflows.
- Consider the timing of payments from customers and suppliers.
- Factor in any loans, investments, or credit lines.

Profit and Loss (Income Statement)

- Compile a detailed profit and loss statement showing your revenue, COGS, and operating expenses.
- Include other income or expenses, such as interest or taxes.
- Calculate the EBIDTA, net profit or loss.

Break-Even Analysis

- Identify your break-even point, where total revenue equals total expenses.
- Calculate the number of units or revenue needed to cover costs.

- Use this analysis to understand when your business will become profitable.

Sensitivity Analysis

- Assess the impact of changes in key variables on your financial projections.
- Conduct sensitivity analyses for factors such as changes in sales volume, pricing, or expenses.
- Understand the potential risks and how they might affect your financial outlook.

Financial Assumptions

- Clearly outline the assumptions you have made when creating your projections.
- Detail the basis for your sales forecasts, expense estimates, and other key financial metrics.
- Be transparent about your assumptions to build credibility.

Tips for Financial Projections

Financial projections are critical and key to

- Understand the business and its viability
- Do a what-if analysis
- Work out the investment requirement
- Work out the critical indicators like break-even point, etc.

A spreadsheet is a perfect tool for making financial projections and performing all kinds of what-if analyses.

A sample sheet is available to the founders for downloading and working on it.

https://shorturl.at/nHctV

FORMATION, LEGAL AND REGULATORY

Business Registration and Legal Requirements

Company Registration

Registering a company in India is a crucial step for startups as it provides legal recognition, protection, and various benefits. A general overview of the process and its importance is given below.

Choose the Business Structure

Decide on the type of business structure, such as a Private Limited Company, Limited Liability Partnership (LLP), Sole Proprietorship, or Partnership.

Unique Name Approval

Propose a unique name for your company and check its availability with the Ministry of Corporate Affairs (MCA). The name should comply with the Companies Act 2013 guidelines.

Digital Signature Certificate (DSC) and Director Identification Number (DIN)

Obtain a Digital Signature Certificate for the directors and apply for Director Identification Numbers.

Drafting Memorandum and Articles of Association

Prepare the Memorandum of Association (MOA) and Articles of Association (AOA) defining the company's objectives and rules for internal management.

Filing with Registrar of Companies (ROC)

File the incorporation documents, including MOA, AOA, and other necessary forms, with the ROC.

Payment of Fees

Pay the prescribed fees based on the company's authorised capital.

Verification and Approval

The ROC will verify the documents and, upon satisfaction, issue the Certificate of Incorporation.

PAN and TAN Application

Apply for the company's Permanent Account Number (PAN) and Tax Deduction and Collection Account Number (TAN).

Compliance with Other Registrations

Obtain Goods and Services Tax (GST) registration, if applicable. Also, comply with other industry-specific, region-specific regulations.

Company Registration is Important

Legal Recognition

Company registration provides legal recognition to your business entity, establishing it as a separate legal entity distinct from its owners.

Limited Liability Protection

In structures like a Private Limited Company or LLP, the liability of the owners is limited to their share capital, protecting personal assets from business debts.

Ease of Doing Business

A registered company can easily enter into contracts, acquire assets, and engage in various business activities.

Access to Funding

Investors, banks, and financial institutions prefer to deal with registered entities, making it easier for startups to attract funding.

Brand Building and Trust

Registered companies often gain more credibility and trust among customers, suppliers, and partners, enhancing the brand image.

Tax Benefits

Registered companies are eligible for various tax benefits and incentives provided by the government.

Perpetual Existence

A registered company has perpetual existence, ensuring continuity even if the ownership or management changes.

Market Presence

Registration helps in establishing a market presence and allows the company to participate in various government and private tenders.

It is advisable to seek professional assistance from a company secretary or a legal expert to ensure compliance with all regulations during the registration process.

Registration for Getting Official Recognition and Startup Status

The **Department for Promotion of Industry and Internal Trade (DPIIT)** registration in India is primarily related to obtaining recognition as a startup under the Startup India initiative. Please note that regulations and processes may change, so it is advisable to check the latest guidelines on the official website or consult with an incubation centre for the most up-to-date information.

Steps for DPIIT Registration

Check Eligibility Criteria

Ensure that your startup meets the eligibility criteria defined by the DPIIT. Typically, startups should be incorporated as a private limited company, partnership firm, or limited liability partnership (LLP). The business should be working towards innovation, development, or improvement of products, processes, or services or have a scalable business model with a high potential for employment generation or wealth creation.

Business Incorporation

Choose a suitable legal structure such as a private limited company, partnership, or LLP.

Register on the Startup India Portal

Go to the Startup India portal (https//www.startupindia.gov.in/ or https//www.nsws.gov.in/) and create an account. Fill in the required details about your startup.

Online Document Submission

Prepare and submit the necessary documents, including the Certificate of Incorporation/Registration, a brief about your business, and other relevant documents.

Self-Certification

Self-certify that your startup meets the specified criteria. The self-certification process involves declaring that your startup is working towards innovation, development, deployment, or commercialisation of new products, processes, or services driven by technology or intellectual property.

Recognition Number

Upon successful verification, you will receive a recognition number for your startup. This recognition provides various benefits and exemptions under different regulations.

Avail Benefits

Startups recognised by DPIIT can avail of various benefits, including tax exemptions, faster exit processes, and eligibility for government schemes.

Compliance

Ensure that you comply with the ongoing reporting requirements and any changes in the guidelines to maintain your startup's recognition.

Benefits of DPIIT Registration

Recognition by the Department for Promotion of Industry and Internal Trade (DPIIT) under the Startup India initiative brings several benefits to eligible startups. These benefits are designed to encourage growth, encourage innovation, and create a favourable environment for startups to thrive. These are some of the key benefits:

Tax Benefits

- Eligibility for a three-year tax holiday in the first 7 years of incorporation, excluding MAT (Minimum Alternate Tax).
- Capital gains tax exemption on the sale of residential property and reinvestment in your startup.

Compliance Relief

- Simplified compliance processes and self-certification in certain labour and environmental laws.
- Reduced regulatory burden and inspections.

Faster Exit

A fast-track exit process for startups to wind up operations within 90 days.

Financial Support

- Access to various government schemes and funds that provide financial support to startups.
- Preference in government procurement.

Networking and Collaboration

- Access to a network of mentors, investors, and industry experts through various Startup India programmes and events.
- Opportunities for collaboration with other startups, industry players, and research institutions.

Intellectual Property Rights (IPR) Support

- Fast-tracking of patent applications and a rebate in patent filing fees.

- Assistance in protecting and managing intellectual property.

Innovation and Research & Development (R&D) Support

- Access to research grants and funds to promote innovation.

- Participation in government-sponsored innovation challenges and competitions.

Market Access

- Inclusion in government-organised startup fairs and events.

- Opportunities to showcase products or services on national and international platforms.

Ease of Doing Business

- Single point of contact for all queries and support through the Startup India Hub.

- Simplified regulatory environment to encourage ease of doing business.

The benefits may evolve, and new initiatives may be introduced over time. Therefore, it is advisable to regularly check the official Startup India portal and stay informed about any updates or changes in the benefits and criteria. Additionally, consult with legal, financial professionals or incubation centre to ensure that you fully understand and leverage the benefits available to your startup.

Co-founders' Agreement

A co-founder agreement is crucial for your startup because it helps establish clear expectations, outlines responsibilities, and mitigates potential conflicts among co-founders. This legal document serves as a foundation for a successful partnership, providing a framework for decision-making, dispute resolution, and the overall governance of the startup.

Importance of a Co-founders' Agreement

Clear Roles and Responsibilities

Define the roles and responsibilities of each co-founder. This helps avoid misunderstandings and ensures everyone is on the same page regarding their contributions to the business.

Equity Distribution

Specify the equity distribution among co-founders. Clearly outline the percentage ownership each co-founder holds and any vesting schedules to incentivise commitment over time.

Decision-Making Processes

Establish decision-making processes. Define how major business decisions will be made, and consider including voting mechanisms or consensus requirements to prevent deadlocks.

Founder Contributions

Outline the contributions of each founder, whether they are financial, intellectual property, or other resources. This ensures that everyone's contributions are acknowledged and protected.

Vesting Schedules

Implement vesting schedules for equity. Vesting encourages co-founders to stay committed to the business over a certain period, typically with a cliff period followed by gradual vesting.

Exit Strategies

Address exit strategies. Determine what happens if a co-founder decides to leave the startup voluntarily or involuntarily and establish buyout mechanisms or procedures for acquiring their shares.

Dispute Resolution

Include a dispute resolution mechanism. Specify how disputes among co-founders will be resolved, whether through mediation, arbitration, or another agreed-upon process.

Non-Compete and Confidentiality

Enforce non-compete and confidentiality clauses. Protect the startup's sensitive information and prevent co-founders from competing directly with the business.

Intellectual Property (IP) Ownership

Clarify IP ownership. Specify that any intellectual property created for the business belongs to the startup, preventing disputes over ownership of key assets.

Founder Departure or Death

Plan for the founder's departure or death. Outline the procedures and implications if a founder decides to leave or in the unfortunate event of a founder's passing.

Key Points to Include

Company Overview

Provide a brief overview of the startup, its mission, and its key objectives.

Founder Information

Detail the names, roles, and responsibilities of each co-founder.

Equity Distribution

Clearly state the initial equity distribution and any conditions or vesting schedules.

Decision-Making Structure

Define the decision-making structure and procedures for major company decisions.

Roles and Responsibilities

Clearly outline the roles and responsibilities of each founder.

Compensation and Benefits

Specify any compensation, salary, or benefits that co-founders may receive.

Founder Contributions

Detail the contributions each founder is making to the startup.

Exit Strategies

Address exit strategies, including buyout options and procedures.

Dispute Resolution

Outline how disputes will be resolved, specifying mediation, arbitration, or other methods.

Confidentiality and Non-Compete

Include confidentiality and non-compete clauses to protect the startup's interests.

IP Ownership

Clearly state the ownership of intellectual property created during the course of the startup.

Founder Departure or Death

Establish procedures for a founder's departure or in case of a founder's death.

Customise the co-founder agreement based on the specific needs and circumstances of your startup. Consulting with legal professionals or startup advisers can provide additional insights and ensure that the agreement meets legal requirements and protects the interests of all co-founders.

Shareholders' Agreement

Importance of a Shareholder Agreement

Governance and Decision-Making

It clarifies the decision-making process within the company, establishing protocols for major business decisions.

Specify voting rights, decision-making thresholds, and procedures for resolving deadlocks.

Equity Ownership and Dilution

It defines the ownership structure, outlines how equity can be transferred, and addresses potential dilution over time.

Outline the initial equity distribution, any anti-dilution provisions, and procedures for the transfer of shares.

Rights and Obligations

It outlines the rights and obligations of each shareholder to avoid misunderstandings.

Define rights to information, participation in major decisions, and obligations to the company.

Dividends and Distributions

This establishes the pattern of profit distribution among shareholders.

Detail dividend policies, distribution mechanisms, and any restrictions on distributions.

Exit Strategies

It addresses scenarios such as the sale of the company or the exit of individual shareholders.

Outline procedures for selling shares, rights of first refusal, and mechanisms for handling acquisition offers.

Buy-Sell Agreements

It provides a mechanism for shareholders to sell their shares in certain circumstances.

Include buy-sell provisions specifying triggering events (e.g., death, disability) and the process for valuation and purchase of shares.

Pre-Emptive Rights

This grants existing shareholders the right to purchase additional shares before they are offered to external parties.

Define pre-emptive rights and any conditions under which they can be exercised.

Confidentiality and Non-Compete

This is for the protection of the company's sensitive information and prevents shareholders from competing directly with the business.

Include confidentiality and non-compete clauses to safeguard the company's interests.

Dispute Resolution

Outlines procedures for resolving disputes among shareholders.

Specify dispute resolution mechanisms, such as mediation or arbitration, to avoid litigation.

Board Composition and Management

Defines the structure of the board of directors and the management team.

Specify the composition of the board, appointment procedures, and roles of key executives.

Drag-Along and Tag-Along Rights

This addresses scenarios where majority shareholders want to sell the company (drag-along) or minority shareholders want to join a sale (tag-along).

Clearly define drag-along and tag-along rights, including conditions and procedures.

Amendments to the Agreement

It outlines the process for making changes to the shareholder agreement.

Specify the procedures and conditions for amending the agreement.

A well-crafted shareholder agreement helps prevent disputes, ensures fair treatment of shareholders, and provides a roadmap for the company's growth and decision-making. It is advisable to seek legal advice when drafting a shareholder agreement to ensure compliance with relevant laws and regulations and to tailor the agreement to the specific needs and circumstances of your startup.

Local Registrations

Navigate the legal landscape by registering your business appropriately. Understand the regulatory framework in India, complying with licensing, permits, and other legal obligations necessary for the smooth operation of your startup.

INTELLECTUAL PROPERTY PROTECTION

Your intellectual property is your creation, and you need to safeguard your ideas and innovations by securing your intellectual property rights. Explore patents, trademarks, and copyrights to protect your unique offerings and establish a competitive edge in the market.

Intellectual property (IP) registration is crucial for your startup as it provides legal protection for your creative and innovative assets. This protection can be essential for securing your competitive advantage, attracting investors, and preventing unauthorised use or reproduction by competitors. In India and internationally, there are specific processes for registering different types of intellectual property.

Importance of Intellectual Property Registration

Protecting Innovations

IP registration safeguards your innovative ideas, inventions, and processes, preventing others from using or profiting from them without your permission.

Brand Protection

Trademark registration protects your brand identity, including names, logos, and slogans, ensuring that consumers associate your products or services with your business.

Market Competitiveness

IP protection can enhance your market competitiveness by establishing exclusive rights to your creations, encouraging innovation, and providing a unique selling proposition.

Attracting Investors and Partnerships

Investors often look for startups with secure intellectual property rights, as it adds value to the company. IP registration can make your startup more attractive for investment and potential partnerships.

Legal Recourse

Registered IP provides a legal foundation for taking legal action against those who infringe on your rights, enabling you to enforce exclusivity and seek damages if necessary.

Intellectual Property Registration in India

Patents

In India, patents are registered with the Indian Patent Office. The process involves filing a patent application, examination by the Patent Office, and, if approved, the granting of the patent.

Trademarks

Trademarks are registered with the Controller General of Patents, Designs, and Trademarks in India. The process includes a comprehensive search, filing the application, examination, and, upon approval, the issuance of a trademark registration certificate.

Copyrights

Copyright registration is done with the Copyright Office in India. The process involves submitting the application along with the required documents, and, upon verification, the issuance of a copyright certificate.

Designs

Design registration is handled by the Controller General of Patents, Designs, and Trademarks. The process includes filing the application, examination, and, upon approval, the registration of the design.

International Intellectual Property Registration

Patents (PCT)

For international patent protection, the Patent Cooperation Treaty (PCT) allows you to file a single international application that is recognised by multiple countries. It simplifies the process of seeking patents in different jurisdictions.

Trademarks (Madrid Protocol)

The Madrid Protocol facilitates the international registration of trademarks. It allows you to file a single application that is recognised by multiple member countries, streamlining the trademark registration process.

Copyrights

Copyright protection is generally automatic in many countries through international conventions. However, some countries may require additional steps for enforcement.

Designs (Hague System)

The Hague System for the International Registration of Industrial Designs allows for the international registration of designs. It simplifies the process of obtaining design protection in multiple countries.

Considerations

Legal Assistance

Consider seeking legal assistance for intellectual property registration to ensure compliance with specific laws and regulations.

Timely Registration

Timely registration is crucial, especially for patents, where the first-to-file principle applies. Early registration can secure your rights and prevent disputes.

Regular Renewal

Keep track of renewal requirements for your registered intellectual property to maintain protection over time.

Intellectual property registration is a strategic step to protect your startup's creations and innovations. Engaging with legal professionals specialising in intellectual property law can help navigate the registration process efficiently and effectively.

COMPLIANCE WITH TAXATION LAWS AND REGULATIONS

Ensure adherence to tax laws, understanding tax structures and liabilities. Establish robust accounting practices to maintain transparency and compliance with financial regulations.

Compliance with taxation laws and regulations is crucial for your startup for several reasons.

Importance of Tax Compliance for Startups

Legal Obligation

Compliance with tax laws is a legal obligation that all businesses, including startups, must adhere to. Failure to comply can result in penalties, fines, and legal consequences.

Financial Management

Proper tax compliance allows for effective financial management. Understanding and fulfilling your tax obligations ensures that your startup's finances are organised and you can avoid unexpected liabilities.

Reputation and Trust

Complying with tax regulations enhances your startup's reputation and builds trust with stakeholders, including customers, investors, and partners. Transparent and ethical tax practices contribute to a positive business image.

Access to Funding

Investors and lenders often scrutinise a startup's financial records, including tax compliance, before providing funding. Demonstrating adherence to tax regulations makes your startup more attractive to potential investors.

Avoidance of Legal Issues

Non-compliance with tax laws can lead to legal issues, audits, and investigations. Adhering to tax regulations helps prevent legal challenges that can be time-consuming and expensive.

Tax Compliance in India

Goods and Services Tax (GST)

GST is a comprehensive indirect tax levied on the supply of goods and services. Startups must register for GST if their turnover exceeds the prescribed threshold.

Income Tax

Startups are subject to income tax on their profits. It is essential to file annual income tax returns and pay taxes in accordance with the Income Tax Act.

TDS (Tax Deducted at Source)

TDS is applicable when making certain payments, such as salaries, interest, or contractor payments. Startups must deduct TDS and comply with related reporting requirements.

Corporate Tax

Private limited companies in India are subject to corporate tax. It is crucial to comply with corporate tax regulations and file annual returns.

Other Local Taxes

Depending on the nature of your business and location, there may be other local taxes and levies that need to be complied with.

International Tax Compliance

Transfer Pricing

For startups involved in international transactions, transfer pricing rules come into play. These rules ensure that transactions between related entities are conducted at arm's length, preventing tax evasion.

Double Taxation Treaties

If your startup operates in multiple countries, consider the implications of double taxation. Many countries have treaties to avoid double taxation on the same income.

Compliance with Local Laws

Understand and comply with the tax laws of each country where your startup has a presence or conducts business activities.

Permanent Establishment (PE)

Be aware of the concept of a permanent establishment, as it may impact your tax obligations in foreign jurisdictions.

Steps for Tax Compliance

Registration

Register for applicable taxes, such as GST and corporate tax, as required by local laws.

Record Keeping

Maintain accurate financial records, including income, expenses, and transactions, to support tax filings.

Filing Returns

Timely file all required tax returns, including income tax returns, GST returns, and any other applicable filings.

Payment of Taxes

Ensure timely payment of all taxes due. Late payments can lead to penalties and interest.

Seek Professional Assistance

Consider seeking professional advice from tax experts or consultants to ensure accurate compliance with complex tax regulations.

Stay Informed

Keep abreast of changes in tax laws and regulations that may affect your startup. Regularly review compliance requirements to stay informed.

Compliance with taxation laws is an ongoing process that requires diligence and proactive management. Consulting with tax professionals or hiring a qualified accountant can provide valuable guidance and support in navigating the complexities of tax compliance, both domestically and internationally.

FUNDRAISING

This chapter is well detailed in which crucial information about the following is given:

Details of fundraising, types of funds, stages of fundraising, various preparations required to be done in advance before the fundraising stage, investors, negotiations, term sheet, etc.

Fundraising is a pivotal aspect of a startup's journey, often serving as the lifeblood that fuels growth and innovation. While the allure of securing funding can be compelling, the process demands a comprehensive understanding and meticulous attention to detail. Being well-informed about fundraising avenues, such as venture capital, angel investors, or crowdfunding platforms, empowers startups to navigate the complex landscape effectively.

Grasping the finer details of fundraising, including valuation methodologies, term sheets, and investor expectations, is paramount. Such insights not only facilitate strategic decision-making but also enhance credibility and trustworthiness in the eyes of potential investors. Ultimately, a startup's success in fundraising hinges on its ability to articulate a compelling vision backed by a thorough comprehension of the financial intricacies and market dynamics.

Determining the right stage for dilution through fundraising is a delicate balance between achieving growth objectives and preserving equity. Typically, startups consider dilution when they have validated their product or service, demonstrated market traction, and require capital to scale operations or enter new markets.

At this juncture, dilution can be strategic, enabling access to resources, expertise, and networks that propel the company forward while maintaining a reasonable ownership stake for founders and early investors.

Careful consideration is essential when selecting an investor to minimise risk and maximise strategic alignment. Startups should prioritise investors who not only bring capital but also offer value beyond monetary contributions. Assessing an investor's track record, industry expertise, network, and long-term vision is crucial. Additionally, founders should conduct thorough due diligence, seek references, and engage in open communication to ensure alignment of goals, values, and expectations. Choosing the right investor can significantly impact a startup's trajectory, influencing its growth, culture, and long-term success.

FUNDAMENTALS OF FUND RAISING FOR STARTUPS

Securing funding is a critical aspect of launching and growing a startup. Various types of funding options are available to entrepreneurs, each with its own set of characteristics, advantages, and considerations. Understanding these options is essential for startups to make informed decisions about their financial future.

Bootstrapping

Bootstrapping is a method of funding a startup using personal savings or revenue generated by the business itself. It is a self-reliant approach that allows entrepreneurs to maintain full control over their venture without seeking external investments. Bootstrapping also helps in avoiding debt or equity dilution, as the startup funds itself. Moreover, it encourages financial discipline and prudent spending, as the entrepreneurs are accountable for every dollar spent.

Having said that, bootstrapping has its limitations. Startups that rely on bootstrapping may have limited resources, which can restrict the speed of growth compared to funded counterparts. Without external investment, the startup's growth trajectory might be slower, and it may take longer to reach milestones.

Friends and Family

Friends and family funding involves raising capital from personal contacts such as friends and family members. This funding option offers easier access to capital, as it relies on personal relationships rather than institutional investors. Friends and family investors may also offer more flexible terms compared to traditional investors. Additionally, entrepreneurs may benefit from the emotional support of close relations, which can be invaluable during the early stages of the startup.

However, raising funds from friends and family can strain personal relationships if the business faces challenges. Failure to repay investments can create tension and conflict within personal relationships. Moreover, friends and family investors may lack expertise in evaluating business opportunities, which could pose a risk to the startup if investments are made without proper due diligence.

Angel Investors

Angel investors are high-net-worth individuals who invest their own money in startups in exchange for equity. They provide quick access to capital, mentorship, and industry expertise. Angel investors are often willing to take risks on early-stage startups and can offer valuable guidance to entrepreneurs based on their own experiences.

One of the main advantages of angel investors is their willingness to provide not only financial support but also mentorship and industry connections. However, it is important to note that angel investors often seek involvement in business decisions and may require a significant equity stake in return for their investment. Entrepreneurs must be prepared to cede some control over their startups in exchange for funding from angel investors.

Venture Capital (VC)

Venture capital involves institutional funds managed by venture capital firms, which are invested in startups in exchange for equity. Venture capital provides startups with significant capital injection, networking opportunities, and guidance from experienced investors. VC funding is often sought by startups that have already demonstrated growth potential and scalability.

While venture capital can provide startups with the resources they need to accelerate growth, it also comes with some drawbacks. Accepting VC funding typically results in the dilution of ownership, as the venture capital firm takes a significant equity stake in the startup. Additionally, venture capitalists have high expectations for growth and returns, and the funding process can be complex and time-consuming.

Crowdfunding

Crowdfunding is a funding method that involves raising small amounts of money from a large number of people via online platforms. It offers startups access to a broad investor base, validation of the product or idea, and the potential for widespread exposure. Crowdfunding can be an effective way for startups to raise capital without giving up equity or taking on debt.

However, crowdfunding can be time-consuming to manage, as startups must create and promote a compelling campaign to attract investors. Additionally, startups must comply with regulatory requirements when soliciting investments from the public. Fulfilling rewards or promises made to crowdfunding backers can also be challenging, as startups must deliver on their commitments in a timely manner.

Corporate Venture Capital (CVC)

Corporate Venture Capital involves investment from large corporations directly or through their venture arms. This funding option offers startups strategic partnerships, access to industry insights, and potential acquisition opportunities. Corporate venture capitalists can provide startups with valuable resources and expertise to help them scale their businesses.

You must consider possible conflicts of interest when accepting funding from corporate venture capitalists. The corporate parent may have its own agenda and priorities, which may not always align with those of the startup. Additionally, startups may face pressure to prioritise the interests of the corporate parent over their own strategic objectives.

Government Grants and Subsidies

Government grants and subsidies are funding provided by government agencies to support startups. This funding option offers startups non-dilutive capital, recognition, and support for innovative projects. Government grants and subsidies can provide startups with the resources they need to develop new products, expand into new markets, and create jobs.

However, startups must meet strict eligibility criteria and navigate lengthy application processes to secure government funding. Competition for grants and subsidies can be fierce, as many startups are vying for limited resources. Additionally, startups must comply with reporting requirements and use the funds for their intended purpose as specified by the government agency.

Accelerators and Incubators

Accelerators and incubators are programmes that provide funding, mentorship, and resources to startups in exchange for equity. These programmes offer startups intensive support, mentorship, and access to a network of experts.

Accelerators and incubators can help startups accelerate their growth and achieve key milestones.

Participating in an accelerator or incubator programme typically involves equity dilution and structured programme commitments. Startups must be willing to cede some control over their businesses in exchange for the resources and support provided by the accelerator or incubator. Additionally, startups must compete for acceptance into these programmes, as competition for spots in top-tier accelerators and incubators can be fierce.

Debt Financing

Debt financing involves borrowing money with the obligation to repay over time with interest. This funding option allows startups to retain ownership without diluting equity. Debt financing can be an attractive option for startups that want to maintain control over their businesses while accessing the capital they need to grow.

One of the main advantages of debt financing is that it allows startups to retain ownership and control over their businesses. Startups are not required to give up equity in exchange for debt financing, which means they can maintain full control over their strategic decisions. Additionally, interest payments on borrowed capital may be tax-deductible, providing additional financial benefits to startups.

Debt financing also comes with some drawbacks. Startups must be prepared to meet repayment obligations, which can put a strain on their cash flow. Additionally, startups must pay interest on the borrowed capital, which can increase their overall cost of capital. Finally, debt financing often requires collateral, which means startups must be willing to put up assets as security for the loan.

Each type of funding has its own set of implications, and the choice depends on your startup's stage, goals, and the industry it operates in. You may well like to use a combination of these funding sources to meet their financial needs.

Fundraising Strategies at Various Stages

Choosing the right funding strategies at different stages of your startup is a critical decision that requires careful consideration of your business goals, market conditions, and growth trajectory.

THE STAGES OF FUNDING FOR START-UPS

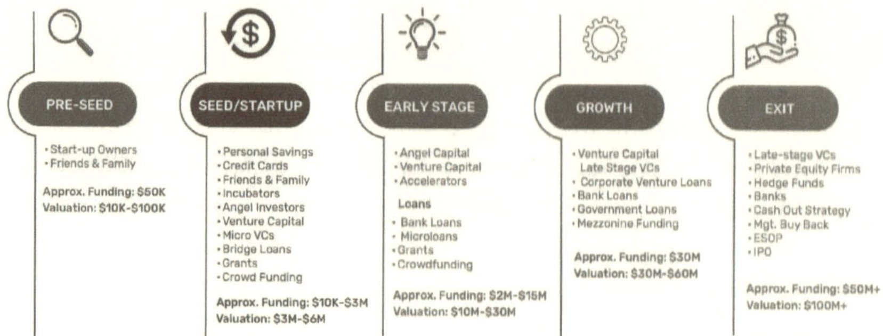

In the idea and concept stage, prioritise bootstrapping to maintain control and focus on proving the viability of your concept as you move into prototype development, leveraging grants and subsidies to fund innovation and early product development.

When seeking market validation, crowdfunding can not only provide capital but also serve as a powerful tool for engaging with potential customers. In the early growth phase, turn to angel investors who bring not just funding but valuable industry insights and networks.

As your startup scales, venture capital becomes a strategic choice to fuel rapid expansion. Joining accelerators during this phase can amplify your growth with additional support and mentorship.

Strategic partnerships become crucial for accessing resources and market channels during expansion, while debt financing may be considered for working capital needs.

When contemplating global expansion or exit strategies, international investors and IPOs can provide the capital required for significant leaps or offer liquidity for investors and founders. Regularly reassess these strategies, considering the evolving needs and circumstances of your startup.

Idea and Concept Stage

- Funding Source: Bootstrapping

- Strategy: Use personal savings or funds generated from a part-time job to develop a proof of concept. Focus on building an MVP and validating the market need for your idea.

Prototype Development

- Funding Source: Grants and Subsidies
- Strategy: Explore government grants, industry-specific subsidies, or startup competitions that support early-stage innovation. Use these funds to develop a prototype and gather initial data on your product's feasibility.

Market Validation

- Funding Source: Crowdfunding
- Strategy: Launch a crowdfunding campaign to raise funds and validate market demand. Leverage the campaign to engage with potential customers, gather feedback, and refine your product.

Early Growth and Traction

- Funding Source: Angel Investors
- Strategy: Seek investment from angel investors who are interested in early-stage startups. Look for investors who not only provide capital but also bring industry expertise and a network that can help accelerate your growth.

Scale-Up and Acceleration

- Funding Source: Venture Capital
- Strategy: Pursue venture capital funding to fuel rapid growth and scale operations. Look for VCs with a track record in your industry, and emphasise the scalability and potential return on investment.

Incubators and Accelerators

- Funding Source: Accelerators
- Strategy: Apply to join reputable startup accelerators. These programmes offer funding, mentorship, and networking opportunities. Accelerators can help refine your business model, provide valuable guidance, and prepare you for the next funding rounds.

Strategic Partnerships for Expansion

- Funding Source: Corporate Partnerships

- Strategy: Explore strategic partnerships with established companies in your industry. These partnerships can provide funding, access to resources, and distribution channels. Look for partners aligned with your growth objectives.

Debt Financing for Working Capital

- Funding Source: Debt Financing

- Strategy: Consider debt financing if your startup has predictable cash flows or working capital needs. This can include traditional bank loans or alternative lending options.

Expansion

- Funding Source: International Investors

- Strategy: If your startup is ready for global expansion, seek investments from international investors who understand the nuances of different markets. Their insights and connections can be valuable assets.

Mature Growth and Exit Planning

- Funding Source: IPO or Acquisition

- Strategy: Explore the possibility of going public through an Initial Public Offering (IPO) or consider acquisition offers from larger companies. This stage aims for a significant liquidity event for early investors and founders.

Adapt this framework based on your specific circumstances and industry dynamics. Additionally, regularly reassess your funding strategy as your startup evolves, and be agile in adjusting your approach based on market feedback and opportunities.

PREPARATIONS FOR FUNDING

As the startup landscape continues to evolve, the journey of raising funding has become increasingly complex and competitive. In this dynamic environment, startup founders must navigate a myriad of factors and considerations to successfully secure the capital needed to fuel their growth and realise their vision.

From establishing strong foundations in compliance and governance to crafting compelling business models and demonstrating exponential scaling potential, each aspect of the fundraising process plays a critical role in shaping investor perception and driving investment decisions.

In this chapter we will deep-dive into the intricacies of raising funding as a startup founder, providing detailed insights and actionable strategies to navigate the fundraising landscape effectively. By addressing key factors such as hygiene factors, team dynamics, track records, business models, unit economics, exponential scaling, and sunrise sectors, startup founders can enhance their fundraising efforts and maximise their chances of securing investment from potential investors.

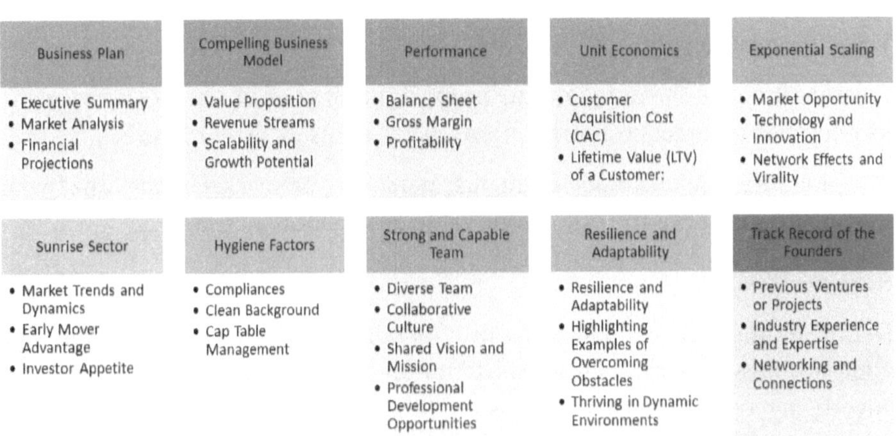

Business Plan

Executive Summary

Provide a concise overview of your startup's vision, mission, objectives, and key milestones in the executive summary.

Summarise the market opportunity, competitive landscape, value proposition, target market, and revenue model to give investors a quick understanding of the business opportunity.

Market Analysis

Conduct thorough market research to analyse industry trends, market dynamics, customer needs, and competitive landscape.

Identify market gaps, unmet needs, or emerging opportunities that your startup can capitalise on to gain a competitive advantage.

Financial Projections

Develop detailed financial projections, including income statements, cash flow forecasts, and balance sheets, to demonstrate the startup's revenue potential, profitability, and financial sustainability.

Use realistic assumptions and data-driven analysis to justify revenue projections, cost estimates, and investment requirements over the short, medium, and long term.

Compelling Business Model

Value Proposition

Clearly articulate the unique value proposition of your product or service and its relevance to target customers' needs, pain points, or aspirations.

Identify key customer segments, personas, or market niches that your startup aims to serve and tailor your value proposition accordingly.

Revenue Streams

Define multiple revenue streams or monetisation strategies that align with your business model, such as subscription fees, licensing, transaction fees, advertising, or affiliate partnerships.

Conduct thorough pricing analysis and market research to determine optimal pricing strategies that maximise profitability while remaining competitive in the market.

Scalability and Growth Potential

Assess the scalability and growth potential of your business model by evaluating factors such as market size, addressable market opportunity, customer acquisition channels, and expansion strategies.

Highlight any competitive advantages, barriers to entry, or network effects that enable your startup to capture market share and sustain long-term growth.

Performance

Balance Sheet

The financial results are a true reflection of the performance and a data-driven, data-targeted working. The balance sheet (with profit and loss statement) should be well-detailed and periodically drawn.

Gross Margin

Calculate the gross margin for each product or service offering by subtracting the cost of goods sold (COGS) from total revenue.

Monitor gross margin trends and identify opportunities to optimise production costs, procurement processes, and supply chain management to improve profitability.

Unit Economics

Customer Acquisition Cost (CAC)

Calculate the cost of acquiring each customer, including marketing expenses, sales commissions, and customer acquisition campaigns.

Monitor CAC trends over time and optimise customer acquisition channels to improve efficiency and maximise return on investment.

Lifetime Value (LTV) of a Customer

Estimate the lifetime value of each customer by projecting their total revenue contribution over the customer lifecycle, including repeat purchases, cross-selling, and upselling opportunities.

Compare LTV to CAC to ensure positive unit economics and sustainable profitability for each customer segment.

Exponential Scaling

Market Opportunity

Identify and quantify the market opportunity for your startup's products or services, including total addressable market (TAM), serviceable addressable market (SAM), and target market segments.

Showcase the scalability of your business model by demonstrating its potential to capture a significant market share and generate exponential revenue growth over time.

Technology and Innovation

Highlight any technological innovations, proprietary algorithms, or intellectual property that give your startup a competitive edge and enable rapid scaling.

Showcase examples of how your technology platform or solution can scale seamlessly to support increasing demand, user growth, and transaction volume.

Network Effects and Virality

Leverage network effects, virality, and word-of-mouth marketing to drive user adoption, engagement, and retention.

Design your product or service to encourage social sharing, referrals, and community building to amplify its reach and impact across users and generate exponential growth.

Sunrise Sector

Market Trends and Dynamics

Stay informed about emerging trends, market shifts, and industry disruptions within sunrise sectors that present significant growth opportunities.

Conduct market research and industry analysis to identify promising sectors with high demand, high valuations, low competition, and potential for innovation and disruption.

Early Mover Advantage

Position your startup as an early mover or pioneer within a sunrise sector to capitalise on first-mover advantages, establish market leadership, and shape industry standards.

Showcase how your startup's products, services, or technologies address unmet needs, solve pressing challenges, or leverage emerging trends within the chosen sector.

Investor Appetite

Research investor appetite and preferences for investing in sunrise sectors, such as venture capital funds, angel investors, corporate venture arms, and strategic investors.

Tailor your pitch and investment thesis to align with investor interests, highlighting the growth potential, market opportunity, and competitive advantage of your startup within the chosen sector.

Hygiene Factors

In the competitive world of startup fundraising, paying attention to hygiene factors is crucial for attracting investors and building long-term success. Hygiene factors encompass various aspects of startup management, including compliance, maintaining a clean background, and managing the cap table effectively. Here is a detailed look at how these factors can impact fundraising:

Compliances

For startups seeking investment, ensuring compliance with legal and regulatory requirements is not just good practice but a necessity. Investors want to see that the startup operates within the bounds of the law and mitigates potential legal risks. This includes understanding and adhering to company registration, tax obligations, data protection laws such as GDPR, industry-specific regulations, and licensing requirements.

Having all necessary agreements in place, including those with co-founders, shareholders, employees, and NDAs, demonstrates professionalism and protects the interests of the startup and its stakeholders.

Clean Background

Investors place a significant emphasis on the integrity and trustworthiness of the startup's founders and key team members. Conducting thorough background checks on co-founders and key team members is essential to identify any potential legal or ethical issues that could raise red flags for investors. Transparency is key here.

Startups should be open with investors about any past challenges or controversies and demonstrate how they have been addressed or resolved. Upholding high ethical standards and integrity in all business dealings is crucial for building trust with investors and securing funding.

Cap Table Management

A well-managed cap table is vital for startups looking to attract investment. Investors want to see an accurate and up-to-date record of equity ownership, including shares allocated to founders, employees, advisers, and previous investors. Using cap table management software or professional services can help startups track equity transactions, equity dilution, and ownership changes accurately.

Transparent communication of the cap table structure to investors and stakeholders is essential to avoid misunderstandings or disputes. Investors need to have confidence in the startup's financial and ownership structure before committing their capital.

Paying attention to these hygiene factors is essential for startups seeking to raise funds. By ensuring compliance, maintaining a clean background, and managing the cap table effectively, startups can build trust with investors, mitigate legal risks, and set themselves up for fundraising success.

Strong and Capable Team

Identifying Key Skills and Expertise: When assembling your team, make sure to identify the key skills and expertise required to drive your startup's growth and success. Look for individuals with technical proficiency, industry knowledge, leadership experience, and a background in entrepreneurship.

Building a Diverse Team

It is essential to build a diverse team with complementary skill sets. This includes expertise in technology development, product management, marketing, sales, finance, and operations.

Emphasising Relevant Experience: Highlight the relevant experience, accomplishments, and contributions of each team member to previous projects or ventures. Investors will want to see that your team has a track record of success and can bring valuable experience to the table.

Developing a Collaborative Culture

Creating a Collaborative Environment: Work to create a collaborative and inclusive team culture that encourages open communication, creativity, and innovation. This will help to develop a positive work environment and drive your team towards common goals.

Promoting a Shared Vision and Mission

Promote a shared vision and mission that aligns with your startup's goals and values. This will help to inspire your team members and ensure that everyone is working towards the same objectives.

Providing Professional Development Opportunities

Provide opportunities for professional development, mentorship, and continuous learning to empower your team members and enable their career growth. Investing in your team in this way will not only benefit them but also your startup as a whole.

Demonstrating Resilience and Adaptability

Showing Resilience and Adaptability

Demonstrate resilience, adaptability, and problem-solving skills in navigating challenges and setbacks. Investors want to see that your team can overcome obstacles and adapt to changes in the market.

Highlighting Examples of Overcoming Obstacles

Showcase examples of how your team has overcome obstacles by pivoting in response to market feedback and iterating on product development. This will demonstrate your team's ability to adapt and evolve in order to achieve success.

Thriving in Dynamic Environments

Highlight your team's ability to thrive in dynamic and uncertain environments. Investors want to know that your team can embrace change as an opportunity for growth and improvement.

By focusing on building a strong and capable team, developing a collaborative culture, and demonstrating resilience and adaptability, you'll be well-positioned to attract investors and drive the success of your startup.

Track Record of the Founders

Previous Ventures or Projects

Highlight any previous entrepreneurial ventures, startups, or projects that founders have been involved in, emphasising successes, milestones, and lessons learned.

Showcase evidence of leadership, innovation, and execution skills demonstrated in previous ventures, such as product launches, revenue growth, customer acquisition, and strategic partnerships.

Industry Experience and Expertise

Emphasise the founders' domain expertise, industry knowledge, and professional experience relevant to the startup's market and sector.

Showcase any accolades, awards, publications, or thought leadership contributions that demonstrate the founders' credibility and expertise in their field.

Networking and Connections

Leverage founders' networks, connections, and relationships within the industry to access resources, opportunities, and strategic partnerships.

Highlight endorsements, testimonials, or referrals from industry peers, mentors, advisers, or investors who can vouch for founders' integrity, capabilities, and track record.

By incorporating these detailed insights into your fundraising strategy, startup founders can effectively navigate the fundraising process, build investor confidence, and secure the necessary capital to fuel their growth and success. Each point plays a crucial role in positioning the startup for success and attracting investment from potential investors who share the startup's vision and believe in its potential to disrupt markets, drive innovation, and create value for stakeholders.

ADVICE ON INVESTMENT

Startups often require significant financial investment to fuel their growth and development. However, seeking investment is a critical decision that comes with its own set of challenges and risks. While securing funding can be a milestone for a startup, it is essential to approach the process with caution and foresight. In this chapter, we'll discuss the points of caution that startups should consider when seeking investment, as well as the ideal stages at which startups should look for investment.

Points of Caution When Seeking Investment in a Startup

Valuation

Avoid Over-valuation

Startups should be cautious about overvaluing their company. An unrealistic valuation can deter potential investors and make it difficult to secure funding.

Thorough Market Research

Conduct thorough market research and financial analysis to determine a fair and reasonable valuation. Consider factors such as market size, competition, growth potential, and revenue projections.

Equity Distribution

Avoid Over-Dilution

Startups should be cautious about giving away too much equity too early. Diluting ownership can reduce the founders' control over the company and impact their ability to make key decisions.

Negotiate Fair Terms

Negotiate fair terms when offering equity to investors. Consider factors such as the percentage of equity offered, the rights and privileges of investors, and any potential restrictions or obligations.

Alignment of Vision and Values

Seek investors who align with the startup's vision, values, and long-term goals. Look for investors who can provide more than just financial backing, such as expertise, industry connections, and strategic guidance.

Research Potential Investors

Conduct due diligence on potential investors. Research their track record, reputation, investment portfolio, and level of involvement with other startups. Ensure compatibility with the startup's objectives and culture.

Terms and Conditions

Thorough Review and Negotiation

Thoroughly review and negotiate the terms and conditions of any investment deal. Pay close attention to factors such as the valuation, equity stake, investment amount, investor rights, and any potential restrictions or obligations.

Seek Legal Advice

Seek legal advice to ensure that the terms of the investment deal are fair and favourable to the startup. Consult with experienced legal professionals who specialise in startup financing and venture capital.

Due Diligence

Conduct Due Diligence

Perform due diligence on potential investors. Research their background, track record, reputation, and investment history. Verify the investor's ability to provide the promised funding and support.

Prepare Due Diligence Materials

Prepare comprehensive due diligence materials to provide to potential investors. This may include financial statements, business plans, market analysis, customer testimonials, and other relevant documents.

Legal and Regulatory Compliance

Ensure Compliance

Ensure that the startup is compliant with all relevant legal and regulatory requirements before seeking investment. This includes company registration, intellectual property protection, tax obligations, and compliance with securities laws.

Consult Legal Experts

Consult with legal experts to ensure that the startup's legal and regulatory obligations are met. Work with experienced attorneys who specialise in startup law and can provide guidance on compliance issues.

Exit Strategy

Develop a Clear Exit Strategy

Have a clear exit strategy in place before seeking investment. Whether through acquisition, IPO, or other means, a well-defined exit strategy demonstrates to investors that the startup is focused on long-term growth and profitability.

Communicate Exit Strategy to Investors

Clearly communicate the startup's exit strategy to potential investors. Provide details on how and when investors can expect to realise a return on their investment, whether through a sale of the company or other means.

By carefully considering these points of caution, startups can increase their chances of securing funding and achieving long-term success. Taking the time to conduct thorough research, negotiate fair terms, and ensure legal and regulatory compliance can help startups build strong relationships with investors and position themselves for growth and profitability.

Stage for a Startup to Look for Investment

The ideal stage at which a startup should seek investment depends on several factors, including the nature of the business, its growth trajectory, and its funding requirements. Generally, startups typically seek investment at one of the following stages:

Seed Stage

At the seed stage, startups are typically in the early stages of development. They may have a prototype MVP but have not yet generated significant revenue. Seed funding is used to validate the business idea, develop the product, and conduct market research.

Early Stage

Startups at the early stage have developed a viable product or service and are beginning to generate revenue. Early-stage funding is used to scale the business, acquire customers, and expand operations. At this stage, startups may seek investment from angel investors, venture capital firms, or crowdfunding platforms.

Growth Stage

Startups at the growth stage have achieved product-market fit and are experiencing rapid growth. Growth-stage funding is used to accelerate expansion, enter new markets, and increase market share. At this stage, startups may seek investment from venture capital firms, private equity investors, or strategic investors.

Later Stage

Startups at the later stage have achieved significant scale and are on the path to profitability. Later-stage funding is used to further scale the business, optimise operations, and prepare for a potential exit. At this stage, startups may seek investment from private equity firms, institutional investors, or through an initial public offering (IPO).

Seeking investment is a critical milestone for startups, but it is essential to approach the process with caution and foresight. By carefully considering the points of caution outlined in this chapter and understanding the ideal stage at which to seek investment, you can improve your chances of securing funding and achieving long-term success.

Decision to Raise Investment

Deciding whether to raise investment is a critical decision for any startup. Here are steps to help you determine whether raising investment is the right choice for your startup:

Assess Your Funding Needs

Evaluate Capital Requirements

Determine how much capital your startup needs to achieve its short-term and long-term goals. Consider factors such as product development, marketing and sales, hiring, and operational expenses.

Financial Projections

Create detailed financial projections to estimate your startup's funding requirements over the next 12-24 months. Consider different growth scenarios and their associated funding needs.

Evaluate Growth Opportunities

Market Potential

Assess the size and growth potential of your target market. Identify opportunities for growth and expansion, including entering new markets, launching new products or services, and scaling operations.

Competitive Landscape

Evaluate your startup's competitive position and identify areas where additional funding can help you gain a competitive advantage. Consider factors such as proprietary technology, unique market positioning, and intellectual property.

Validate Your Business Model

Proof of Concept

Validate your business idea and demonstrate that there is demand for your product or service. Gather feedback from potential customers, test your product or service in the market, and refine your business model based on the results.

Revenue Generation

Start generating revenue as soon as possible. Focus on acquiring paying customers and building a scalable business model that can support future growth.

Consider Timing and Market Conditions

Market Timing

Assess whether market conditions are favourable for fundraising. Consider factors such as investor interest in your industry or sector, overall economic conditions, and investor sentiment.

Investor Landscape

Research potential investors and assess their appetite for investment in startups like yours. Consider factors such as the size of their investment portfolio, investment criteria, and track record.

Develop a Clear Investment Strategy

Define Your Objectives

Clearly define your objectives for raising investment. Determine how the funds will be used to support your startup's growth and development.

Identify Potential Investors

Research potential investors and identify those who are a good fit for your startup. Consider factors such as their industry expertise, investment philosophy, and track record.

Prepare Your Pitch

Create a Compelling Pitch Deck

Develop a comprehensive pitch deck that highlights your startup's value proposition, market opportunity, competitive advantage, and financial projections. Clearly articulate why investors should invest in your startup.

Practice Your Pitch

Practice your pitch until you can deliver it confidently and effectively. Anticipate questions that investors may ask and prepare thoughtful responses.

Evaluate Funding Options

Consider Different Funding Sources

Explore different funding sources, including angel investors, venture capital firms, crowdfunding platforms, and government grants. Evaluate the pros and cons of each option and choose the one that best aligns with your startup's needs and objectives.

Assess the Risks and Rewards

Risk Assessment

Evaluate the risks associated with raising investment, including dilution of ownership, loss of control, and investor expectations. Consider whether the potential benefits outweigh the risks.

Return on Investment

Assess the potential return on investment for your startup and its investors. Consider factors such as the startup's growth potential, market opportunity, and competitive advantage.

Make an Informed Decision

Consult with Advisers

Seek advice from experienced entrepreneurs, advisers, and mentors who can provide guidance and support. Consider joining startup accelerators or incubators that can provide resources and networking opportunities.

Due Diligence

Conduct thorough due diligence on potential investors and funding sources. Research their track record, reputation, investment portfolio, and level of involvement with other startups.

Monitor and Manage Investor Relationships

Communication

Keep investors informed about your startup's progress, challenges, and milestones. Establish open and transparent communication channels to build trust and confidence.

Manage Expectations

Manage investor expectations and provide realistic updates on your startup's performance and growth trajectory. Be proactive in addressing any concerns or issues that may arise.

By following these steps and carefully evaluating your startup's funding needs, growth opportunities, and market conditions, you can make an informed decision about whether raising investment is the right choice for your startup.

Criteria for Choosing Investor/s

Investor Compatibility

Alignment of Vision and Values

Seek investors who share your startup's vision and values. Look for investors who are passionate about your industry and believe in your mission. Ensure that the investor understands and supports your long-term goals for the company.

Investor Expertise

Look for investors who have relevant experience and expertise in your industry. Consider investors who have successfully built, scaled, or exited companies similar to yours. Evaluate whether the investor can provide valuable insights, connections, and guidance to help your startup succeed.

Track Record and Reputation

Investor Track Record

Research the investor's track record of successful investments. Look for investors who have a history of backing successful startups and generating positive returns for their portfolio companies. Consider the investor's track record of adding value beyond capital, such as strategic guidance and introductions to potential customers or partners.

References and Recommendations

Seek references and recommendations from other entrepreneurs who have worked with the investor.

Ask about the investor's level of involvement, communication style, and the value they added to the startup. Verify the investor's reputation and credibility within the startup community.

Investment Terms and Conditions

Fair Valuation

Ensure that the valuation offered by the investor is fair and reasonable. Conduct market research and financial analysis to determine a fair valuation for your startup. Avoid overvaluing your company, as this can deter potential investors and make it difficult to secure funding.

Equity Stake

Consider the percentage of equity that the investor is asking for in exchange for their investment.

Be cautious about giving away too much equity too early, as this can dilute your ownership and control over your company.

Negotiate a fair and equitable equity split that aligns with the investor's contribution and the startup's future growth potential.

Investment Amount

Evaluate whether the investment amount offered by the investor aligns with your startup's funding needs. Consider the capital required to achieve key milestones, such as product development, market expansion, and customer acquisition.

Ensure that the investment amount is sufficient to support your startup's growth and development plans.

Investor Involvement and Expectations

Level of Involvement

Clarify the level of involvement that the investor expects to have in your startup.

Discuss how often you will communicate, what decisions require investor approval, and how you will work together to achieve your goals.

Set clear expectations for the investor's role, responsibilities, and contributions to the startup.

Long-Term vs. Short-Term Goals

Ensure that the investor's goals align with your startup's long-term vision and objectives.

Avoid investors who are only interested in short-term gains and quick exits.

Seek investors who are committed to supporting your startup's growth and success over the long term.

Due Diligence

Perform Due Diligence

Conduct thorough due diligence on potential investors. Research the investor's background, track record, reputation, and investment history. Verify the investor's ability to provide the promised funding and support.

Check References

Seek references from other entrepreneurs who have worked with the investor. Ask about their experience, level of involvement, and the value they added to the startup. Verify the investor's reputation and credibility within the startup community.

Legal and Regulatory Compliance

Legal Advice

Seek legal advice to ensure that the terms of the investment deal are fair and favourable to your startup. Consult with experienced attorneys who specialise in startup financing and venture capital. Ensure that the investment deal complies with all relevant legal and regulatory requirements.

Compliance with Regulations

Ensure that the investment deal complies with securities laws, tax regulations, and any other applicable laws and regulations. Consult with legal experts to ensure that the investment agreement protects your startup's interests and rights.

Exit Strategy

Clear Exit Strategy

Have a clear exit strategy in place before accepting investment. Consider different exit options, such as acquisition, IPO, or secondary sale.

Communicate your exit strategy to potential investors and provide clarity on how and when they can expect to realise a return on their investment.

Communication with Investors

Keep investors informed about your startup's progress, challenges, and milestones. Establish open and transparent communication channels to build trust and confidence.

Manage investor expectations and provide realistic updates on your startup's performance and growth trajectory.

By carefully considering these points and conducting thorough due diligence, startup founders can find the right investor who not only provides financial support but also adds value to the startup through expertise, connections, and strategic guidance.

NEGOTIATIONS WITH INVESTORS

Negotiating with investors is a critical step for startup founders to secure the funding needed to grow and scale their businesses. Effective negotiation allows founders to achieve favourable terms, including valuation, investment amount, equity stake, and investor rights while maintaining the long-term health and viability of their startup.

By carefully navigating the negotiation process, founders can establish a strong and mutually beneficial relationship with their investors, ensuring alignment of interests and a shared vision for the future success of the company.

Negotiations with investors are not only about securing capital but also about building trust, ushering in transparency, and laying the foundation for a successful partnership that will support the startup's growth and development in the years to come.

Valuation

Market Comparables

Research the valuations of similar startups in your industry and geographic location. Use this data as a benchmark for negotiating your startup's valuation.

Consider factors such as revenue, growth rate, market size, and competitive landscape when comparing valuations.

Financial Projections

Prepare detailed financial projections that justify your startup's valuation. Use conservative assumptions and realistic growth estimates to support your valuation.

Provide evidence of past performance and future growth potential to justify your valuation to investors.

Negotiation Strategy

Develop a negotiation strategy that takes into account your startup's unique value proposition, growth potential, and funding requirements.

Be prepared to justify your valuation to investors with data, market research, and financial projections.

Investment Amount

Funding Needs

Determine the amount of funding your startup needs to achieve its short-term and long-term goals. Consider factors such as product development, market expansion, and customer acquisition.

Prepare a detailed budget that outlines how the investment will be used and the expected return on investment for the investor.

Negotiation Strategy

Develop a negotiation strategy that takes into account your startup's funding requirements and growth plans. Be prepared to justify the investment amount to investors based on your startup's financial projections, market opportunity, and competitive landscape.

Equity Stake

Founder Ownership

Consider the percentage of equity that you and your co-founders are willing to give up in exchange for the investment. Balance the investor's equity stake with your ownership and control over the company.

Negotiation Strategy

Develop a negotiation strategy that maximises your ownership stake while still attracting investment.

Be prepared to negotiate the investor's equity stake based on your startup's valuation, funding requirements, and growth potential.

Investor Rights and Privileges

Board Seats

Consider whether the investor will have a seat on your startup's board of directors and what rights and responsibilities they will have. Negotiate the number of board seats, voting rights, and decision-making authority that the investor will have.

Veto Rights

Discuss any veto rights that the investor may have over key decisions such as hiring/firing executives, entering into major contracts, or raising additional funding. Ensure that any veto rights are reasonable and in the best interests of your startup.

Liquidation Preferences

Negotiate the investor's liquidation preference, which determines how proceeds from a sale or liquidation of the company are distributed. Ensure that the liquidation preference is fair and equitable for both founders and investors.

Vesting Schedule

Founder Commitment

Implement a vesting schedule for founder equity to ensure that founders are committed to the long-term success of the startup. Consider a four-year vesting schedule with a one-year cliff period before any equity vests.

Investor Commitment

Consider whether the investor's equity should be subject to a vesting schedule to align their interests with those of the founders. Negotiate a vesting schedule that reflects the investor's commitment to the long-term success of the startup.

Due Diligence

Investor Background

Conduct due diligence on the investor to ensure that they are a good fit for your startup.

Research the investor's background, track record, reputation, and investment history.

Reference Checks

Seek references from other entrepreneurs who have worked with the investor to verify their credibility and reputation. Ask about their experience, level of involvement, and the value they added to the startup.

Legal and Regulatory Compliance

Ensure that the investment agreement complies with all relevant legal and regulatory requirements.

Seek advice from experienced attorneys who specialise in startup financing and venture capital.

Communication and Relationship Building

Trust and Transparency

Build a strong and transparent relationship with the investor based on trust, communication, and mutual respect. Keep the investor informed about your startup's progress, challenges, and milestones.

Regular Updates

Provide regular updates to the investor on your startup's performance, growth, and financials.

Establish open communication channels to address any concerns or issues that may arise.

Long-Term Relationship

Prioritise building a long-term relationship with the investor based on shared goals, objectives, and values. Focus on building trust and credibility with the investor to ensure a successful partnership.

Exit Strategy

Clear Exit Plan

Have a clear exit strategy in place before accepting investment and communicate it clearly to the investor. Consider different exit options, such as acquisition, IPO, or secondary sale.

Negotiate Fair Terms

Negotiate fair and reasonable terms for the investor's exit, including liquidation preferences, redemption rights, and drag-along rights. Ensure that the exit strategy aligns with your startup's long-term goals and objectives.

Be Prepared to Walk Away

Know Your Limits

Set a bottom line for the negotiation and be prepared to walk away if the terms are not favourable.

Avoid making concessions out of desperation or fear of losing the investment.

Prioritise Long-Term Success

Prioritise the long-term success and sustainability of your startup over short-term gains or concessions.

Focus on negotiating terms that are fair and equitable for both parties and protect the interests of your startup.

By being careful and considering these points during negotiations with investors, startup founders can secure the funding they need while protecting the interests and long-term success of their startup.

Tips on Negotiating with Investors

Comprehensive Preparation

Know Your Business Inside Out

Understand your startup's business model, market opportunity, competitive landscape, and financials in detail. Anticipate questions investors may ask and prepare thoughtful, data-driven responses.

Research Your Investors

Understand the investor's investment thesis, portfolio companies, industry focus, and track record.

Tailor your pitch and negotiation strategy to align with the investor's interests and objectives.

Understand Market Dynamics

Stay up-to-date with market trends, industry benchmarks, and comparable valuations.

Use market data to support your valuation and negotiation stance.

Set Clear Objectives

Define Your Goals

Clearly define your objectives for the negotiation, including the amount of funding needed, valuation, and terms of the investment deal. Determine your walk-away point and be prepared to negotiate within a certain range.

Prioritise Your Objectives

Rank your negotiation objectives in order of importance and focus on achieving the most critical ones. Be willing to compromise on less critical objectives to achieve your top priorities.

Lead with Your Strengths

Articulate Your Value Proposition

Clearly articulate what sets your startup apart from the competition and why investors should be excited about the opportunity.

Highlight your unique technology, market traction, customer testimonials, or other competitive advantages.

Showcase Traction and Milestones

Provide evidence of market validation, such as customer acquisitions, revenue growth, partnerships, or product milestones.

Demonstrate that your startup is making tangible progress and is well-positioned for future growth.

Be Transparent and Authentic

Build Trust and Rapport

Be open, honest, and transparent throughout the negotiation process.

Address any concerns or challenges upfront and propose solutions to mitigate them.

Establish a Relationship

Focus on building a strong and mutually beneficial relationship with the investor.

Demonstrate that you are committed to the long-term success of your startup and value the investor as a strategic partner.

Listen Actively

Understand Investor Needs

Listen carefully to the investor's questions, concerns, and objectives.

Tailor your pitch and negotiation strategy to address their specific needs and interests.

Be Open to Feedback

Be open to feedback and constructive criticism.

Use it as an opportunity to improve your pitch and strengthen your negotiation position.

Be Flexible

Negotiate in Good Faith

Approach the negotiation with a spirit of collaboration and mutual benefit.

Be open to compromise and creative solutions that satisfy both parties.

Focus on Win-Win

Look for opportunities to create value for both your startup and the investor.

Find common ground and build on areas of agreement to reach a mutually beneficial outcome.

Stay Calm and Confident

Manage Emotions

Stay calm, composed, and professional during the negotiation.

Avoid getting emotional or defensive, even if faced with difficult questions or objections.

Project Confidence

Believe in the value of your startup and project confidence in your pitch and negotiation strategy.

Demonstrate that you are a capable and trustworthy entrepreneur who is capable of leading the company to success.

Be Prepared to Walk Away

Know Your Limits

Set clear boundaries and be prepared to walk away if the terms are not favourable.

Do not be afraid to turn down an offer that doesn't align with your startup's goals and values.

Maintain Leverage

Demonstrate that you have alternative options and are not desperate for funding.

This will give you more leverage in the negotiation and help you secure better terms.

Get Professional Help

Legal and Financial Advice

Seek advice from experienced professionals, such as startup lawyers and financial advisers, to help you navigate the negotiation process.

They can help you review term sheets, negotiate terms, and ensure that your interests are protected.

Consult with Mentors

Seek guidance from experienced entrepreneurs and mentors who have been through the fundraising process before.

Learn from their experiences and insights, and use them to inform your negotiation strategy.

Follow-Up

Provide Additional Information

If the investor requests additional information or clarification during the negotiation, provide it promptly and professionally.

Address any outstanding questions or concerns to move the negotiation forward.

Stay Engaged

Maintain open communication with the investor even after the negotiation is complete.

Keep them updated on your startup's progress, milestones, and any significant developments.

By following these tips and tricks, startup founders can negotiate effectively with investors and secure the funding they need to grow and scale their businesses.

NEGOTIATING A TERM SHEET

Negotiating a term sheet is a critical step in securing funding for your startup. Here's a detailed breakdown of the points of contention, points of fallout, points of hard negotiations, and points to be careful about during the negotiation process.

Points of Contention

Valuation

Founder Perspective

Founders often aim for a higher valuation to retain a larger ownership stake and maintain control over the company.

Investor Perspective

Investors seek a lower valuation to maximise their equity stake and potential return on investment.

Mitigation Strategies

Comparable Analysis

Conduct thorough research on comparable companies and recent transactions in your industry to justify your startup's valuation.

Market Potential

Highlight the market opportunity, growth potential, and competitive advantages of your startup to justify a higher valuation.

Flexibility

Be open to negotiation and compromise. Consider alternative valuation methods or structures, such as convertible notes or SAFE agreements, to bridge the valuation gap.

Equity Stake

Founder Perspective

Founders want to retain as much equity as possible to maintain control and incentivise team members.

Investor Perspective

Investors seek a significant equity stake in exchange for their investment to align their interests with the success of the startup.

Mitigation Strategies

Negotiation

Negotiate a fair and equitable equity split that reflects your startup's valuation, funding requirements, and growth potential.

Vesting Schedule

Implement a vesting schedule for founder equity to align the interests of founders and investors and incentivise long-term commitment and performance.

Alignment

Emphasise the importance of aligning incentives and ensuring that all stakeholders are committed to the long-term success of the startup.

Investment Amount

Founder Perspective

Founders seek a larger investment to fuel growth, expand operations, and achieve key milestones.

Investor Perspective

Investors want to limit their exposure and risk by investing an amount that aligns with their investment criteria and funding strategy.

Mitigation Strategies

Funding Requirements

Clearly articulate your startup's funding requirements and the rationale behind the requested investment amount.

Financial Projections

Provide evidence of market demand, revenue growth, and future projections to support your funding needs and justify the investment amount.

Flexibility

Be open to negotiation and compromise. Consider structuring the investment in multiple tranches or stages based on the achievement of key milestones.

Investor Rights and Privileges

Founder Perspective

Founders may be reluctant to grant investors significant rights and privileges that could impact their autonomy and control over the company.

Investor Perspective

Investors seek certain rights and privileges, such as board seats, veto rights, and liquidation preferences, to protect their investments and influence key decisions.

Mitigation Strategies

Negotiation

Negotiate investor rights and privileges that are fair and reasonable for both parties. Consider the investor's level of involvement, expertise, and value-add to the startup.

Governance Structure

Ensure that the investment terms and governance structure protect the interests of both founders and investors while allowing the startup to maintain flexibility and agility.

Points of Fallout

Valuation

Potential Fallout: If founders and investors cannot agree on a fair valuation, the negotiation may reach an impasse, leading to a breakdown in the negotiation process.

Mitigation Strategies

Flexibility

Be open to compromise and creative solutions that satisfy both parties. Consider alternative valuation methods or structures to bridge the valuation gap.

Market Data

Use market data, financial projections, and comparable company valuations to support your valuation and negotiate based on data and evidence.

Equity Stake

Disagreements over the equity split and ownership stake may lead to tension and conflict between founders and investors.

Mitigation Strategies

Clear Communication

Clearly communicate your startup's ownership structure and the rationale behind the proposed equity split. Be willing to negotiate and find a mutually acceptable solution.

Alignment

Emphasise the importance of aligning incentives and ensuring that all stakeholders are committed to the long-term success of the startup.

Investment Amount

Potential Fallout

If founders and investors cannot agree on the investment amount, the negotiation may break down, leaving the startup without the funding needed to grow.

Mitigation Strategies

Justification

Clearly articulate your startup's funding requirements and the rationale behind the requested investment amount. Provide evidence of market demand, revenue growth, and future projections.

Flexibility

Be open to negotiation and compromise. Consider structuring the investment in multiple tranches or stages based on the achievement of key milestones.

Investor Rights and Privileges

Potential Fallout

Disputes over investor rights and privileges may lead to a breakdown in trust and communication between founders and investors.

Mitigation Strategies

Fairness

Negotiate investor rights and privileges that are fair and reasonable for both parties. Consider the investor's level of involvement, expertise, and value-add to the startup.

Transparency

Clearly define the investor's rights and privileges in the term sheet and ensure that they align with the startup's long-term goals and objectives.

Points of Hard Negotiations

Valuation

Hard Negotiation

Determining a fair valuation for the startup is often one of the most challenging aspects of the negotiation process.

Mitigation Strategies

Research

Conduct thorough research on comparable companies and recent transactions in your industry to justify your startup's valuation.

Flexibility

Be open to compromise and creative solutions that satisfy both parties. Consider alternative valuation methods or structures to bridge the valuation gap.

Equity Stake

Hard Negotiation

Negotiating the equity split between founders and investors requires careful consideration and compromise.

Mitigation Strategies

Communication

Clearly communicate your startup's ownership structure and the rationale behind the proposed equity split. Be willing to negotiate and find a mutually acceptable solution.

Alignment

Emphasise the importance of aligning incentives and ensuring that all stakeholders are committed to the long-term success of the startup.

Investment Amount

Hard Negotiation

Determining the investment amount requires balancing the startup's funding needs with the investor's risk tolerance and investment criteria.

Mitigation Strategies

Justification

Clearly articulate your startup's funding requirements and the rationale behind the requested investment amount. Provide evidence of market demand, revenue growth, and future projections.

Flexibility

Be open to negotiation and compromise. Consider structuring the investment in multiple tranches or stages based on the achievement of key milestones.

Investor Rights and Privileges

Hard Negotiation

Negotiating investor rights and privileges requires balancing the investor's desire for control and influence with the startup's need for autonomy and decision-making authority.

Mitigation Strategies

Negotiation

Negotiate investor rights and privileges that are fair and reasonable for both parties. Consider the investor's level of involvement, expertise, and value-add to the startup.

Transparency

Clearly define the investor's rights and privileges in the term sheet and ensure that they align with the startup's long-term goals and objectives.

Points to Be Careful About

Legal and Regulatory Compliance

Mitigation Strategies

Legal Review

Be careful to ensure that the term sheet complies with all relevant legal and regulatory requirements.

Professional Advice

Seek advice from experienced attorneys who specialise in startup financing and venture capital to review the term sheet and ensure that your startup's interests are protected.

Investor Reputation and Track Record

Mitigation Strategies

Due Diligence

Conduct thorough due diligence on the investor's background, track record, and reputation.

Reference Checks

Seek references from other entrepreneurs who have worked with the investor to verify their credibility and reputation within the startup community.

Long-Term Relationship

Mitigation Strategies

Communication

Prioritise open communication, trust, and transparency to ensure a successful partnership that benefits both parties in the long term.

Alignment

Emphasise the importance of aligning incentives and ensuring that all stakeholders are committed to the long-term success of the startup.

Exit Strategy

Mitigation Strategies

Planning

Be careful to have a clear exit strategy in place before finalising the term sheet.

Negotiation: Consider different exit options, such as acquisition, IPO, or secondary sale, and negotiate fair and reasonable terms for the investor's exit.

By carefully considering these points during the negotiation process, you can navigate the negotiation effectively, secure the funding needed to grow and scale your businesses and establish a strong and mutually beneficial relationship with your investors.

CREATING A COMPELLING PITCH DECK

Craft a visually appealing and informative pitch deck that communicates your startup is value proposition, market potential, and financial projections. Highlight key metrics, competitive advantages, and the team is expertise to capture the interest of potential investors.

While approaching angel investors, venture capitalists, and other funding sources, tailor your approach to different funding sources, understanding their preferences and expectations. Build relationships with angel investors and venture capitalists through networking, pitch events, and strategic introductions.

Making a Pitch Deck

Start with a Compelling Introduction

1. Provide a brief overview of the startup's mission, vision, and the problem it aims to solve.

2. Include a compelling tagline or elevator pitch that encapsulates the essence of your startup's value proposition.

3. Introduce the founding team members with photos highlighting their relevant experience, skills, and achievements.

Define the Problem and Solution

1. Clearly articulate the pain points or challenges faced by your target audience or market segment.

2. Use real-life examples, anecdotes, or case studies to illustrate the severity and significance of the problem.

3. Introduce your solution and explain how it effectively addresses the identified problem, emphasising its unique selling points and benefits to customers.

Showcase the Market Opportunity

1. Conduct thorough market research to quantify the size, growth rate, and dynamics of your target market.

2. Segment the market into relevant categories or customer segments to demonstrate the addressable market opportunity.

3. Provide insights into emerging trends, market gaps, or underserved niches that present opportunities for your startup to capitalise on.

Explain the Business Model

1. Clearly articulate how your startup generates revenue and sustains its operations.

2. Describe the pricing strategy, revenue streams, and monetisation model employed by your startup.

3. Discuss any recurring revenue streams, subscription plans, or value-added services that contribute to the business model's scalability and long-term viability.

Highlight Traction and Milestones

1. Showcase key traction metrics and milestones achieved by your startup, such as user growth, revenue milestones, product launches, or strategic partnerships.

2. Use visual aids such as charts, graphs, or infographics to present traction data in a clear and compelling manner.

3. Highlight any notable achievements or validation from customers, industry experts, or media outlets.

Present the Product or Technology

1. Provide a comprehensive overview of your product or technology, highlighting its features, functionalities, and unique selling points.

2. Include screenshots, product demos, or prototypes to showcase the user interface and user experience.

3. Explain any technical innovations, proprietary algorithms, or intellectual property that differentiate your product from competitors.

Outline the Go-to-Market Strategy

1. Describe your startup's go-to-market strategy, including customer acquisition channels, distribution channels, and marketing tactics.

2. Discuss the target customer segments, buyer personas, and customer acquisition cost (CAC) estimates for each channel.

3. Highlight any partnerships, collaborations, or strategic alliances that enhance your go-to-market strategy and accelerate customer acquisition.

Address the Competitive Landscape

1. Conduct a thorough analysis of the competitive landscape, identifying direct and indirect competitors, their strengths, weaknesses, and market positioning.

2. Showcase your startup's competitive advantages, differentiation strategies, and barriers to entry that give it a sustainable competitive edge.

3. Provide insights into the market share, customer preferences, and competitive dynamics within your industry or market segment.

Discuss the Financial Projections

1. Present detailed financial projections, including revenue forecasts, expense breakdowns, profit margins, and cash flow projections.

2. Use historical data, market trends, and growth assumptions to justify the financial forecasts and demonstrate the startup's growth trajectory.

3. Include sensitivity analysis or scenario planning to account for potential risks, uncertainties, or market fluctuations.

Articulate the Ask

1. Clearly state the amount of funding you are seeking, along with the intended use of funds and investment timeline.

2. Provide details on the investment terms, valuation methodology, and equity stake offered to investors.

3. Explain the potential return on investment (ROI) for investors and the value proposition of partnering with your startup.

Include a Compelling Conclusion

1. Summarise the key takeaways from your pitch deck, reinforcing the startup's value proposition, market opportunity, and investment thesis.

2. End with a strong call to action, encouraging investors to engage further with your startup and explore investment opportunities.

3. Express gratitude for investors' time and consideration, inviting them to reach out for follow-up discussions or meetings.

Additional Tips

1. Tailor the pitch deck to your target audience, customising the messaging and content to address their specific interests, concerns, and preferences.

2. Keep the pitch deck concise and focused, prioritising the most relevant and compelling information while avoiding unnecessary details or jargon.

3. Keep additional explanation and detailing slides ready for further detailing if required.

4. Start with a short story which inspired you to conceptualise your startup. It can be a real-life story or a made-up one as an example to illustrate the problem statement.

5. Use compelling visuals, storytelling techniques, and data-driven insights to engage investors and make your pitch memorable.

6. Practice delivering the pitch with confidence and enthusiasm, refining your presentation skills to effectively convey your passion and conviction.

Solicit feedback from mentors, advisers, or peers to iterate and improve the pitch deck iteratively, ensuring clarity, coherence, and effectiveness.

By incorporating these detailed insights and best practices into your pitch deck creation process, you can create a compelling and persuasive presentation that captivates investors' attention, communicates your startup's value proposition, and maximises your chances of securing investment for your venture.

The Knack of Making Powerful Pitching

Start with a Compelling Introduction

Begin with a captivating title story that connects to your problem statement, that grabs the audience's attention. Have a great origin story, how the idea occurred to you. Avoid starting with too much detail or technical jargon right away, as it may overwhelm the audience.

Define the Problem and Solution

Clearly articulate the problem your startup solves and how your solution addresses it. Oversimplify the problem or downplay its significance; investors want to understand the market needs for your startup addresses.

Showcase the Market Opportunity

Provide market research and data to support the size and growth potential of your target market.

Exaggerated market size or growth projections without credible evidence can undermine your credibility.

Explain the Business Model

Clearly outline your revenue streams, pricing strategy, and scalability. Overcomplicating the business model or unrealistic revenue projections should be avoided.

Highlight Traction and Milestones

Showcase key achievements, such as customer acquisitions, partnerships, or revenue milestones. Relying solely on future projections should be avoided; investors want to see evidence of progress and momentum.

Present the Product or Technology

Provide a demo or visual representation of your product to illustrate its functionality and value. Refrain from getting bogged down in technical details; focus on how your product solves a problem for the end user.

Outline the Go-to-Market Strategy

Articulate a clear plan for acquiring customers and penetrating the market. Do not underestimate the importance of marketing and sales strategies in driving adoption and growth.

Address the Competitive Landscape

Acknowledge competitors and explain how your startup differentiates itself. Dismiss or ignore competitors should be avoided; investors want to see that you understand the competitive landscape.

Discuss the Financial Projections

Provide realistic financial projections based on sound assumptions and data. Do not inflate revenue projections or underestimate expenses; be transparent and conservative in your estimates.

Articulate the Ask

Clearly state the amount of funding you're seeking and how it will be used. Be not vague or ambiguous about your funding needs; investors appreciate clarity and transparency.

Include a Compelling Conclusion

End with a strong closing slide that reinforces your key points and call to action. Avoid rushing through the conclusion or leaving investors with unanswered questions; make sure to summarise the main takeaways and invite further discussion.

Tips for Delivering Presentations

1. Practice your pitch multiple times to ensure smooth delivery and timing.
2. Constantly adjust your pitch to be suitable as per the audience.
3. Have different size pitches and stories, for different kind of audience.
4. Read directly from the slides; engage with the audience.
5. Maintain eye contact, use hand gestures and a confident body language. Move around.
6. Have a firm and polite tone of voice.
7. Simple words, no jargon.
8. Draw analogies
9. Use visuals, don't tell
10. Be enthusiastic and passionate about your startup; investors are more likely to be convinced if you believe in your vision.
11. Be prepared to answer questions and address objections from investors.
12. Avoid getting defensive or evasive when faced with tough questions; honesty and transparency are key.

START TO BUILD

With the understanding of various primary preparations and the company formation done, it is time to build the startup. In this chapter you will know about the details of team building, fundamentals for creation of the technical solution in the form of MVP and the technology development options.

Team Building

Build an Initial Team

Building the initial team for your startup is a critical step that can significantly impact your company's success.

Define Your Startup's Needs

Clearly understand the roles and skills required for the initial phase of your startup. Identify key functions such as product development, marketing, sales, and operations.

Identify Core Team Members

Start with essential roles, including Founder/CEO. Provide overall leadership and vision.

CTO/Technical Lead. If your startup is tech-focused, having technical expertise is crucial.

Marketing/Sales Lead: Ensure someone is dedicated to promoting and selling your product or service.

Network and Tap into Your Contacts

Leverage your professional network, including former colleagues, industry connections, and mentors. Personal connections can be a valuable source for finding skilled and trustworthy team members.

Consider Co-Founders

Look for co-founders who complement your skills and share your vision. Having co-founders can bring diverse perspectives and distribute responsibilities. Be careful in choosing the right co-founder.

Freelancers and Contractors

Consider hiring freelancers or contractors for specific tasks if you are not ready for full-time employees. This allows flexibility in scaling your team as needed.

Utilise Online Platforms

Use online platforms and job boards to find potential team members. Platforms like LinkedIn, AngelList, and startup-specific job boards can be effective in connecting with talent.

Attend Networking Events

Attend industry-specific events, meetups, alumni meets, and conferences to connect with professionals in your field. Networking can lead to finding individuals interested in joining a startup.

Engage with Startup Communities

Join startup communities and forums both online and offline. Engaging with the startup ecosystem can help you find like-minded individuals who are passionate about entrepreneurship.

Evaluate Skill Sets and Culture Fit

Assess candidates not only for their technical skills but also for their cultural fit with your startup. Shared values and enthusiasm for your mission are crucial in the early stages.

Pitch Your Vision

Clearly articulate your startup's vision and mission when recruiting. A compelling vision can attract individuals who are not just looking for a job but want to be part of something meaningful.

Offer Equity

In the early stages, when financial resources may be limited, consider offering equity or stock options as part of the compensation package. This aligns the team's interests with the success of the startup.

Conduct Informal Interviews

Before making formal offers, conduct informal interviews or meetups to gauge the chemistry and compatibility with potential team members. Personality and communication style are crucial in a startup environment.

Before making formal offers, conduct informal interviews or meetups to gauge the chemistry and compatibility with potential team members. Personality and communication style are crucial in a startup environment.

Start Small and Scale Gradually

Begin with a small core team and scale gradually as your startup grows. This allows you to maintain a tight-knit group in the early stages and expand strategically.

Be Transparent

Be transparent about the challenges and uncertainties of startup life. Honest communication helps set realistic expectations for potential team members.

Build a Collaborative Culture

Develop a collaborative and open culture from the start. Encourage feedback, share responsibilities, and create an environment where everyone feels valued. – Develop and encourage a collaborative and open culture from the start. Encourage feedback, share responsibilities, and create an environment where everyone feels valued.

Invest in Onboarding

Develop an effective onboarding process to help new team members integrate smoothly into the startup and understand their roles.

Building an initial team is a dynamic process that requires adaptability and a keen understanding of your startup's needs. It is about finding individuals who share your passion and vision while bringing diverse skills to contribute to the success of your venture.

Key to Building a Great Team

Hiring the right talent

Develop a comprehensive hiring strategy to attract and retain top talent in the Indian job market. Emphasise cultural fit, skills, and a passion for the company as the mission when recruiting, ensuring a cohesive and motivated team.

Cultivating a Positive Work Culture

Encourage and develop a positive work environment that promotes collaboration, innovation, and employee well-being.

Define and communicate core values, encouraging a shared sense of purpose among team members.

Team Development and Leadership

Invest in continuous training and development programmes to enhance the skills and capabilities of your team.

Develop strong leadership, providing guidance and support to empower your team members and drive collective success.

Acknowledging and Celebrating Achievements, No Matter How Small

The practice of acknowledging and celebrating achievements, regardless of their size, cultivates a positive and motivating work environment.

Celebrating small wins is essential for recognising individual and team efforts, encouraging a culture of appreciation, and building a foundation for sustained success.

This positive reinforcement contributes to higher morale, increased productivity, and a collective sense of accomplishment within the startup.

Boosting Morale and Maintaining a Positive Outlook

Founders play a pivotal role in boosting morale by maintaining a positive outlook, even in the face of challenges.

Cultivating a positive work environment, offering constructive feedback, and expressing gratitude contribute to higher team morale and motivation.

A positive outlook from the founder sets the tone for the entire team, inspiring resilience, creativity, and a shared commitment to overcoming obstacles.

Motivational Techniques

Implementing motivational techniques and practices is essential for maintaining a positive and driven mindset.

Techniques such as goal visualisation, positive affirmations, and structured reward systems contribute to sustained motivation and focus.

Motivational practices help founders navigate challenges with resilience and maintain a proactive approach to achieving startup objectives.

Developing a Positive and Inclusive Company Culture

A positive and inclusive company culture is built on values of respect, diversity, and collaboration.

Encouraging open communication, recognising achievements, and encouraging a sense of belonging contribute to a workplace where everyone feels valued and motivated.

A positive culture is a catalyst for innovation, teamwork, and sustained success in the startup journey.

Encouraging Collaboration and Open Communication Within the Team

Collaboration and open communication are essential for a cohesive and high-performing startup team.

Encouraging a culture where team members freely share ideas, feedback, and concerns develops \ trust and innovation.

Open communication ensures that the entire team is aligned with the startup's goals, contributing to a more effective and motivated workforce.

Motivating Your Team

Inspiring and motivating team members is a crucial leadership skill for founders.

Building a shared vision and a sense of purpose, recognising individual contributions, and providing opportunities for growth contribute to a motivated and engaged team.

Motivating the team develops a positive work environment, enhances productivity, and ensures that everyone is aligned with the startup's objectives.

Inspiring and Motivating Team Members

Inspiring and motivating team members involves effective leadership, clear communication, and developing a sense of shared purpose.

Recognising and celebrating individual and team achievements boosts morale and creates a positive, collaborative work environment.

PRODUCT / SOLUTION / SERVICE DEVELOPMENT AND TECHNOLOGY

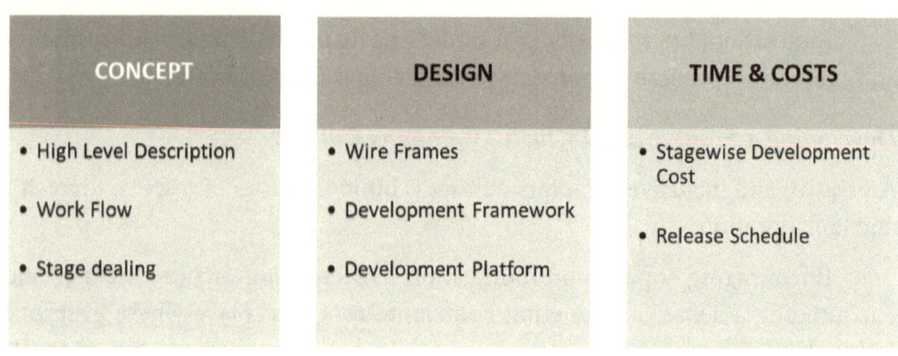

Developing an MVP

Developing a Minimum Viable Product is a crucial step for startups and businesses to test their product hypothesis and gather feedback from users with minimal investment. Here are the various steps to guide you through the process of developing an MVP

Define Your MVP Objectives

Clearly articulate the goals and objectives of your MVP. Identify the core features and functionalities that will be included to test your product concept.

Identify Your Target Audience

Understand your target audience and their needs. Define the user personas and the specific problem or pain point your MVP aims to address.

Conduct Market Research

Research the market to validate your idea and understand the competitive landscape. Analyse existing solutions and identify gaps that your product can fill.

Prioritise Features

Prioritise features based on their importance to the core functionality of your product. Focus on the features that will allow you to test your key hypotheses.

Create a Lean Canvas

Use a Lean Canvas or a similar tool to document key elements of your business model, including customer segments, value propositions, channels, and revenue streams. (Detailed in chapter in this book)

Build a Prototype

Create a low-fidelity prototype to visualise the user interface and flow of your product. This can be a paper prototype, wireframes, or a digital mockup.

Select Development Approach

Decide whether to develop the MVP in-house, outsource development, or use no-code/low-code platforms, depending on your resources, expertise, and budget.

Develop Core Features

Build only the essential features necessary to demonstrate the core functionality of your product. Keep the MVP simple and focused on solving the primary problem.

Iterative Development

Adopt an iterative development approach. Release a basic version of your product quickly, gather feedback, and make continuous improvements based on user insights.

User Feedback and Testing

Collect user feedback through alpha and beta testing. Use feedback to refine and enhance your product. Pay attention to user behaviour, preferences, and pain points.

Metrics and Analytics

Implement analytics tools to track user engagement, retention, and other key metrics. Analyse data to gain insights into user behaviour and make data-driven decisions.

Refine and Pivot

Based on user feedback and data analysis, refine your product by adding features, improving usability, and addressing any issues. Be open to pivoting if necessary.

Prepare for Scale

As you receive positive feedback and see increasing user adoption, prepare to scale your product. Optimise infrastructure, address scalability issues, and plan for a broader user base.

Launch and Market

Once you have a more polished version based on user feedback, officially launch your MVP to a wider audience. Implement marketing strategies to promote your product and attract users.

Monitor and Gather Insights

Continue monitoring user behaviour, gathering insights, and addressing any issues that arise post-launch. Use customer feedback for ongoing improvements.

Plan for Next Iterations

Plan for subsequent iterations and the development of additional features based on user needs, market trends, and your evolving business strategy.

The goal of an MVP is to learn and iterate quickly. Focus on gathering actionable insights, and be willing to make adjustments to your product and business model based on user feedback and market dynamics.

Leveraging Technology for Scalability

Embrace scalable technologies to support your business growth. Invest in robust infrastructure, cloud solutions, and automation to ensure that your technology stack can adapt to increasing demand and evolving requirements.

Balancing Innovation With Market Needs

Strike a balance between innovation and addressing market needs. Stay attuned to customer feedback and market trends while encouraging a culture of creativity and experimentation within your product development team.

PROJECT MANAGEMENT

Developing use case flows is an essential aspect of designing and understanding the user experience within your startup. Several tools can help you create visually appealing and comprehensive use case flows. Here are some recommended tools:

Pen and Paper

Sometimes, the simplest tools are the most effective. Sketching out use case flows on paper allows for quick ideation and iteration.

Draw.io

Type Web-based diagramming tool

Key Features: Free, integrates with various cloud services, supports a wide range of diagram types, including flowcharts and use case diagrams.

Lucid Chart

Collaboration support, extensive template library, real-time editing, and integration with other productivity tools.

Balsamiq

Wireframing tool

Low-fidelity mockups, easy to use, support quick ideation, and suitable for early-stage design.

Miro

Online whiteboard platform

Key Features: Collaborative virtual workspace supports flowcharts, mind maps, wireframes, and real-time collaboration.

Whimsical

Collaborative virtual workspace

Key Features: User-friendly, real-time collaboration, supports flowcharts, wireframes, and mind maps.

Microsoft Visio

Desktop and web-based diagramming tool

Key Features A Rich set of templates integrates with other Microsoft Office applications and is suitable for creating use case diagrams and flowcharts.

Adobe XD

Design and prototyping tool

Key Features: Create interactive prototypes that are suitable for designing and testing user interfaces.

Axure RP

Prototyping tool

Key Features: Advanced prototyping supports dynamic and interactive prototypes and is suitable for detailed design and testing.

Mind Meister

Mind mapping tool

Key Features: Visualise and organise thoughts, which are useful for brainstorming and structuring ideas.

These tools cater to different aspects of the design and planning process. Depending on your startup's specific needs, you may choose a combination of tools for tasks like ideation, wireframing, collaborative planning, and detailed prototyping. It is often beneficial to experiment with a few tools to see which one aligns best with your workflow and requirements.

TECH DEVELOPMENT OPTIONS

In-House Development

Control and Customisation

In-house teams offer maximum control over the development process and allow for tailored solutions.

Deep Understanding

Developers have an in-depth understanding of the product, leading to better alignment with business goals.

Rapid Adjustments

Quick adjustments and changes can be made based on real-time feedback.

Hiring and retaining skilled developers

It can be expensive, especially for startups with budget constraints.

Time-Consuming

Building a team and the product from scratch can take time, delaying time-to-market.

Limited Scalability

In-house teams may face challenges in scaling up or down rapidly based on project needs.

Outsourcing

Cost Savings

Outsourcing to countries with lower labour costs can lead to significant cost savings.

Focus on Core Competencies

Allows the startup to focus on core business activities while experts handle development.

Diverse Skill Sets

Access to a pool of specialised skills without the need for in-house recruitment.

Communication Challenges

Time zone differences and language barriers may lead to communication challenges.

Dependency on External Providers

Reliance on external vendors for critical development components.

Quality Control

Ensuring quality and adherence to standards can be challenging when not directly overseeing the development process.

Choosing an Outsourcing Agency

Define Your Requirements

Clearly define your project requirements, scope, and expected outcomes before approaching outsourcing agencies.

Research and Shortlist

Research potential outsourcing agencies, considering factors such as expertise, experience, client reviews, and portfolio.

Check References

Request and check references from previous clients to gauge the outsourcing agency's performance and reliability.

Assess Skills and Expertise

Evaluate the technical skills and expertise of the outsourcing team to ensure they align with your project needs.

Communication and Collaboration

Assess the agency's communication processes, language proficiency, and ability to collaborate effectively with your in-house team.

Security Measures

Ensure that the outsourcing agency follows robust security measures to protect your intellectual property and sensitive data.

Scalability and Flexibility

Consider the agency's ability to scale resources based on project requirements and adapt to changing needs.

Contractual Terms

Carefully review contractual terms, including project milestones, timelines, payment schedules, and exit clauses.

Visit, if Possible

If feasible, visit the outsourcing agency's office to get a first-hand look at their work environment and meet key team members.

Legal and Compliance Considerations

Ensure the outsourcing agency complies with relevant legal and regulatory requirements, including data protection laws.

Role of a Consultant and Mentor

Consultant

A consultant can provide strategic advice and guidance, helping the startup make informed decisions about technology choices, development processes, and overall business strategy.

They bring industry expertise and can offer insights based on their experience with similar projects.

Consultants can assist in identifying potential challenges and proposing effective solutions.

Mentor

A mentor plays a crucial role in providing guidance and support to entrepreneurs and team members.

They offer valuable insights based on their own experiences, helping the startup navigate challenges and avoid common pitfalls.

Mentors can provide a broader perspective, helping the team see beyond immediate issues and consider long-term goals.

Importance

Both consultants and mentors contribute to your startup's learning and growth, offering external perspectives that can enhance decision-making and problem-solving.

Their guidance can be particularly valuable during critical phases such as technology selection, scaling, and strategic planning.

Mentors, in particular, can contribute to the personal and professional development of individuals within the startup, encouraging a culture of continuous learning.

While in-house development offers control and customisation, outsourcing can provide cost savings and access to diverse skills. Choosing the right outsourcing agency involves thorough research and consideration of various factors. Additionally, the role of a consultant and mentor is crucial for strategic advice, industry insights, and overall guidance in navigating the complexities of technology development and business growth.

GET ROLLING

This chapter is all about marketing, scaling operations, future challenges, social media strategy, etc. Once you are ready with the company and technology, you will need to latch on to the marketing for your product/ service to reach out to customers and start to generate revenue.

MARKETING AND BRANDING

Developing a Marketing Strategy Tailored to the Audience

Understanding the diverse cultural, linguistic, and demographic aspects of the Indian market is crucial for crafting an effective marketing strategy. India is a diverse country with varying cultural norms, languages, and traditions across different regions. To resonate with the local audience, startups need to ensure that their messaging aligns with these unique characteristics.

Market Research and Audience Segmentation

Conduct comprehensive market research to understand the demographics, preferences, and behaviours of your target audience in different regions of India.

Segment the audience based on factors such as age, gender, location, language, and cultural background to tailor marketing messages effectively.

Localisation of Content

Translate marketing materials, including website content, advertisements, and social media posts, into regional languages to reach a wider audience.

Adapt marketing messages to reflect local preferences, values, and traditions, ensuring cultural sensitivity and relevance.

Personalisation and Engagement

Use data analytics and customer insights to personalise marketing communications and offers based on individual preferences and behaviours.

Engage with the audience through interactive content, storytelling, and user-generated content to develop a sense of community and connection.

Utilising Social Media and Digital Marketing

In India, social media usage is widespread, making it an essential channel for reaching and engaging with the target audience. Leveraging social media platforms effectively can help startups build brand awareness and drive customer engagement.

Partnerships and Collaborations for Market Penetration

Form strategic partnerships with local businesses, influencers, or organisations to enhance your market penetration. Collaborate with established entities to leverage their existing customer base and gain credibility in the Indian market.

SCALING OPERATIONS

Scaling Strategies for the Market

Tailor your scaling strategies to the unique dynamics of the market. Consider factors like regional variations, cultural nuances, and diverse consumer behaviours when expanding your operations to ensure sustained growth.

Managing Growth and Scalability Challenges

Anticipate and address challenges associated with rapid growth, such as increased demand, operational complexities, and resource constraints. Implement scalable processes, invest in technology, and optimise workflows to manage growth effectively.

EXPANDING INTO NEW MARKETS WITHIN INDIA

Identify and explore untapped markets within India for expansion. Conduct market research to understand local preferences and adapt your products or services to cater to the specific needs of different regions.

NAVIGATING CHALLENGES

Common Challenges Faced by Startups

Recognise challenges such as regulatory hurdles, intense competition, talent acquisition, and funding constraints that startups commonly face in the Indian ecosystem. Develop proactive strategies to mitigate these challenges and develop resilience.

Strategies for Overcoming Obstacles

Implement adaptive strategies to overcome obstacles, including effective problem-solving, agile decision-making, and continuous learning. Cultivate a culture that embraces challenges as opportunities for innovation and improvement.

Learning from Failure and Adapting to Change

Embrace a mindset that views failures as valuable learning experiences. Encourage a culture of innovation and adaptability, where teams can pivot when necessary and incorporate lessons learned from setbacks into future strategies.

FUTURE TRENDS AND OPPORTUNITIES

Keeping a keen eye on the future is crucial for startups aiming for sustained success in the dynamic Indian startup landscape. To thrive in this ever-evolving ecosystem, it is not enough to merely react to current trends; you must anticipate future developments and position your startup accordingly. Based on the points below, you can delve deeper into emerging trends, identify future opportunities and challenges, and adapt to technological advancements and market shifts:

Understanding Emerging Trends

The Indian startup landscape is a melting pot of innovation, fuelled by advancements in technology, changes in consumer behaviour, and evolving market demands. To stay ahead of the curve, it is essential to stay informed about the latest trends shaping the industry. This includes but is not limited to, the rise of artificial intelligence (AI) and machine learning, the growing importance of sustainability and ethical business practices, the increasing adoption of digital solutions, and the shifting preferences of the modern consumer.

By understanding these trends, you can innovate, adapt, and tailor your offerings to meet the evolving needs and preferences of your target market effectively.

Identifying Future Opportunities and Challenges

Innovation thrives on anticipation. By proactively identifying potential opportunities and challenges on the horizon, you can strategically position your startup for long-term growth. This involves not only analysing current market trends but also forecasting future developments, such as emerging technologies, regulatory changes, and untapped markets.

By keeping a watchful eye on the horizon, you can capitalise on emerging opportunities and mitigate potential risks before they impact your business, thus ensuring the resilience and sustainability of your startup.

Adapting to Technological Advancements and Market Shifts

In today's fast-paced business environment, agility is key to survival. Startups must be responsive to technological advancements and market shifts, adapting their strategies and business models accordingly. Embracing innovation, investing in research and development, and being prepared to pivot are essential elements of this adaptability.

Whether it is adopting new technologies to streamline operations, leveraging data analytics to gain valuable insights, or exploring new market segments to diversify revenue streams, startups must remain flexible and open to change. By doing so, you not only stay relevant but also gain a competitive edge in the market, ensuring the long-term success and sustainability of your startup.

PLATFORM SELECTION AND CONTENT STRATEGY

Identify the most popular social media platforms in India, such as Facebook, Instagram, Twitter, LinkedIn, and YouTube, to focus marketing efforts.

Develop a content strategy tailored to each platform, considering the format, tone, and style that resonates with the audience on each channel.

Targeted Advertising and Influencer Partnerships

Utilise targeted advertising features offered by social media platforms to reach specific audience segments based on demographics, interests, and behaviours.

Collaborate with influencers and content creators who have a strong presence and influence on social media to amplify brand messaging and reach a wider audience.

Partnerships and Collaborations for Market Penetration

Forming strategic partnerships and collaborations with local businesses, influencers, or organisations can significantly enhance market penetration and credibility in India.

Strategic Alliances and Co-Branding

Identify potential partners, such as complementary businesses, industry associations, or community organisations, with whom you can form strategic alliances or co-branding initiatives.

Leverage partner networks and resources to expand your reach, access new customer segments, and strengthen brand credibility in the Indian market.

Influencer Marketing and Affiliate Programmes

Partner with influential individuals or celebrities in India who can endorse your products or services to their followers and fan base.

Implement affiliate marketing programmes to incentivise partners, affiliates, or influencers to promote your offerings and drive customer referrals.

Scaling Operations

Scaling operations in the Indian market requires careful planning and execution to accommodate regional variations, cultural nuances, and diverse consumer behaviours effectively.

Regional Expansion and Localisation

Identify high-growth regions or cities within India where there is demand for your products or services and prioritise expansion efforts accordingly.

Adapt your operations, supply chain, and distribution networks to accommodate regional preferences, regulations, and infrastructure challenges.

Technology Adoption and Automation

Invest in technology solutions, such as cloud-based systems, enterprise resource planning (ERP) software, and customer relationship management (CRM) tools, to streamline operations and scale efficiently.

Implement automation technologies and processes to improve productivity, reduce costs, and enhance scalability across various business functions.

Managing Growth and Scalability Challenges

Rapid growth poses unique challenges for startups operating in the Indian market, including increased demand, operational complexities, and resource constraints.

Capacity Planning and Resource Allocation

Conduct regular capacity planning assessments to anticipate future demand and allocate resources, such as manpower, inventory, and infrastructure, accordingly.

Invest in scalable resources and infrastructure that can accommodate future growth without compromising performance or quality.

Talent Acquisition and Training

Recruit and onboard skilled professionals who can support the company's growth objectives and contribute to its success in the Indian market.

Provide ongoing training and development opportunities to employees to enhance their skills, capabilities, and job satisfaction.

Expanding into New Markets Within India

Identifying and exploring untapped markets within India is essential for sustained growth and market expansion.

Market Segmentation and Targeting

Segment the Indian market based on factors such as demographics, geography, income levels, and psychographics to identify new market opportunities.

Develop targeted marketing strategies and product offerings tailored to the specific needs and preferences of different market segments.

Market Entry Strategies

Evaluate different market entry strategies, such as organic growth, partnerships, acquisitions, or franchising, based on the target market characteristics and business objectives.

Pilot test new market initiatives and offerings in selected regions to assess market demand, viability, and scalability before scaling up operations.

Navigating Challenges

Startups operating in the Indian ecosystem face various challenges, including regulatory hurdles, intense competition, talent acquisition, and funding constraints.

Regulatory Compliance and Risk Management

Stay informed about regulatory requirements, compliance obligations, and industry standards relevant to your business operations in India.

Develop robust risk management strategies and contingency plans to mitigate regulatory, legal, and operational risks effectively.

Competitive Differentiation and Value Proposition

Differentiate your offerings from competitors by highlighting unique features, benefits, and value propositions that resonate with the Indian audience.

Continuously monitor market trends, competitive dynamics, and consumer preferences to identify opportunities for innovation and differentiation.

Strategies for Overcoming Obstacles

Implementing adaptive strategies and developing a culture of innovation and resilience can help startups overcome obstacles and thrive in the Indian market.

Agile Decision-Making and Problem-Solving

Cultivate a culture of agile decision-making, experimentation, and rapid iteration to adapt to changing market conditions and customer needs.

Encourage cross-functional collaboration and brainstorming sessions to generate creative solutions to business challenges and obstacles.

Continuous Learning and Improvement

Develop a learning culture within the organisation that encourages employees to seek feedback, embrace failure as a learning opportunity, and continuously improve their skills and capabilities.

Invest in ongoing training, mentorship, and professional development programmes to empower employees to innovate, grow, and succeed.

Learning from Failure and Adapting to Change

Embracing failure as a valuable learning experience and developing adaptability and resilience are essential for startups operating in the Indian ecosystem.

Failure Analysis and Post-Mortem Reviews

Conduct post-mortem reviews and failure analysis to identify root causes, lessons learned, and actionable insights from past failures and setbacks.

Encourage open and transparent communication, feedback, and knowledge sharing within the organisation to facilitate learning and improvement.

Pivot and Iteration

Be willing to pivot and iterate on your business model, product offerings, or market strategies based on feedback, market dynamics, and changing customer preferences.

Embrace experimentation and innovation as integral components of the startup journey, and iterate rapidly to refine and optimise your approach.

Future Trends and Opportunities

Staying informed about current and emerging trends in the Indian startup ecosystem is crucial for identifying future opportunities and challenges.

Technology Adoption and Innovation

Keep abreast of technological advancements, innovations, and disruptive trends that are reshaping industries and markets in India.

Embrace emerging technologies, such as artificial intelligence, blockchain, and Internet of Things (IoT), to drive innovation, efficiency, and competitive advantage.

Market Disruption and Industry Transformation

Anticipate shifts in consumer behaviour, market dynamics, and industry trends that may present opportunities for disruption or transformation.

ACCIDENT ZONE – POINTS OF FAILURE

> It is important to know the various points on which you need to be careful about, and which leads to several large scale problems and failure of a startup sometimes. It is critical to know upfront, about the points on which you have to be extra vigilant and overcome them.

Embarking on the journey of startup is an exhilarating yet challenging endeavour filled with uncertainty, risk, and opportunity. As startup founders, navigating the path to success requires resilience, resourcefulness, and a willingness to learn from both triumphs and setbacks.

Most startups falter along their journey and offer actionable insights and tips to mitigate these risks. The reasons may be from inadequate research and decision-making in haste to conflicts amongst founders and unforeseen regulatory changes, each potential pitfall presents an opportunity for introspection, adaptation, and growth.

By understanding the root causes of failure and implementing proactive strategies to address them, startups can enhance their resilience, agility, and chances of long-term success.

To a young or seasoned founder, this will be a roadmap to navigate the complexities of the startup landscape with confidence, tenacity, and unwavering determination. Embrace the challenges, seize the opportunities, and embark on a transformative journey of innovation, impact, and enduring success.

POINTS OF FAILURE

Inadequate Research / Subject Knowledge

Starting a business without sufficient market research or expertise in the industry can lead to misconceptions about customer needs, market dynamics, and competitive landscape. Lack of thorough market research can lead to misjudgement of customer needs, competitive landscape, and market trends.

Insufficient subject knowledge may result in flawed assumptions, ineffective strategies, and missed opportunities for innovation. Conduct thorough market research to understand customer pain points, preferences, and buying behaviour. Invest time in gaining subject knowledge through industry networking, attending conferences, and seeking mentorship from experienced professionals.

Continuously monitor market trends, consumer behaviour, and competitive developments to stay informed and adapt your strategy accordingly.

Additional Tips:

- Dive deep into primary and secondary market research to gather insights on customer preferences, pain points, and behaviour.

- Stay updated on industry trends, emerging technologies, and regulatory changes through continuous learning and engagement with industry experts.

Decision in a Hurry

Making critical decisions hastily without careful consideration or analysis can result in costly mistakes, missed opportunities, and strategic missteps. Such decisions may result from external pressures, fear of missing out (FOMO), or lack of confidence in the decision-making process. Hasty decisions can lead to short-sightedness, overlooking critical factors, and neglecting thorough analysis of risks and opportunities.

Take the time to gather relevant information, weigh the pros and cons, and consult with advisers or mentors before making important decisions. Avoid impulsive reactions to market fluctuations or competitive pressures; instead, maintain a strategic focus and long-term perspective.

Implement decision-making frameworks or processes to ensure thoughtful deliberation and consensus-building within the team.

Additional Tips:

- Practice patience and discipline in decision-making, allowing sufficient time for deliberation, evaluation, and consultation with stakeholders.

- Consider seeking diverse perspectives and conducting scenario analysis to assess potential outcomes and implications before making decisions.

Idea's Implementation is Completely Dependent on Getting Investment

Relying solely on external funding to execute your business idea can hinder agility, creativity, and resourcefulness, leading to a lack of sustainability if funding falls through. Overemphasis on fundraising can distract from core business activities, hinder organic growth, and increase vulnerability to market uncertainties.

Relying solely on external funding for idea implementation may indicate a lack of resourcefulness, innovation, and adaptability. Bootstrap or pursue alternative funding sources, such as grants, crowdfunding, or revenue-based financing, to validate your idea and build traction before seeking investment. Focus on creating value and generating revenue from day one rather than waiting for external validation or funding to kickstart operations.

Develop a lean and scalable business model that prioritises efficiency, profitability, and self-sustainability to reduce dependency on external capital.

Additional Tips:

- Bootstrap initial operations using personal savings, revenue from early customers, or low-cost MVP (Minimum Viable Product) development to validate the idea and demonstrate traction.

- Focus on building a sustainable business model that generates value for customers and generates revenue independently of external investment.

Weak Business Value Proposition

Failing to articulate a compelling value proposition that resonates with customers can result in low demand, pricing pressure, and difficulty acquiring and retaining customers. A weak value proposition fails to communicate the unique benefits, differentiation, and relevance of the product or service to target customers.

Lack of clarity or alignment between the value proposition and customer needs can result in low demand, high churn rates, and difficulty in acquiring and retaining customers. Clearly define the unique value proposition of your product or service, emphasising the benefits, differentiation, and value it delivers to customers.

Validate your value proposition through customer feedback, market testing, and iteration to ensure alignment with customer needs and preferences. Continuously refine and communicate your value proposition based on market insights, competitive positioning, and evolving customer expectations.

Additional Tips:

- Conduct customer interviews, surveys, and usability tests to gather feedback and validate the value proposition with target customers.

- Iterate on the value proposition based on customer insights, addressing pain points, highlighting benefits, and refining messaging for clarity and effectiveness.

Compete Against the Biggies

Attempting to compete directly with larger, more established competitors without a clear differentiation strategy or competitive advantage can result in market saturation, pricing pressure, and limited market share. Failure to differentiate or compete effectively against big competitors may result in pricing pressure, commoditisation, and difficulty in gaining market share.

Direct competition with larger, more established players requires careful differentiation, innovation, and agility to carve out a niche and gain traction in the market. Identify niche markets, underserved segments, or specialised needs where you can carve out a unique position and compete effectively against larger players.

Differentiate your offering through innovation, customisation, superior customer service, or unique value-added features that resonate with your target audience. Leverage agility, flexibility, and innovation as strengths to outmanoeuvre larger competitors and capitalise on emerging market opportunities.

Additional Tips:

- Identify areas of underserved demand, niche markets, or specialised customer segments where your startup can offer unique value and outmanoeuvre larger competitors.

- Focus on building strong relationships with customers, delivering exceptional value, and leveraging agility and innovation as competitive advantages.

Redundancy due to Radical Change in the Ecosystem

The redundancy of a startup can often be traced back to the rapid shifts in the ecosystem, particularly when a paradigm change, like the emergence of artificial intelligence, disrupts traditional business models.

In the wake of AI's advancements, many startups find themselves grappling with obsolescence as their once-innovative solutions become overshadowed by AI-driven alternatives. This shift not only renders certain business practices redundant but also necessitates a fundamental re-evaluation of value propositions and operational strategies.

Startups failing to adapt to this new reality risk being left behind, highlighting the imperative of foresight and agility in navigating the ever-evolving landscape of technological innovation.

Tiff Amongst Founders

Conflict or disagreement among co-founders can lead to dysfunction, lack of alignment, and distraction from core business priorities, ultimately undermining team cohesion and performance. Conflict or discord among co-founders can arise from differences in vision, goals, values, or communication styles, leading to dysfunction and breakdown in team dynamics.

Unresolved tensions or disagreements may escalate, causing distraction, demotivation, and, ultimately, dissolution of the founding team. Establish clear roles, responsibilities, and decision-making processes within the founding team to minimise ambiguity and reduce potential conflicts.

Encourage open communication, trust, and mutual respect among co-founders through regular team meetings, transparent discussions, and conflict resolution mechanisms. Seek external mediation or professional guidance if interpersonal conflicts persist and threaten the stability and effectiveness of the founding team.

Additional Tips:

- Establish clear roles, responsibilities, and decision-making frameworks within the founding team to minimise ambiguity and mitigate potential conflicts.

- Develop a culture of open communication, mutual respect, and constructive feedback, creating a supportive and collaborative environment where conflicts can be addressed openly and resolved effectively.

Exit of Key Team Member/s

Losing key team members, especially founders or critical employees, can disrupt operations, erode institutional knowledge, and impact morale, potentially derailing the startup's progress and growth. The departure of key personnel may create uncertainty, hinder productivity, and delay progress on critical initiatives, affecting the startup's ability to execute its strategy effectively.

Implement succession planning and talent development strategies to groom and retain key team members, ensuring continuity and resilience in the event of departures. Cultivate a strong company culture that values teamwork, collaboration, and employee engagement, encouraging loyalty and commitment among team members. Cross-train employees and document critical processes and knowledge to mitigate the impact of key personnel changes and facilitate smooth transitions.

Additional Tips:

- Invest in building a strong organisational culture and sense of belonging, encouraging loyalty, and commitment among team members to reduce turnover and retain talent.

- Develop succession plans, cross-train employees, and document critical processes to mitigate the impact of key personnel changes and ensure business continuity.

Spending Too Much Too Fast

Overspending or misallocating financial resources without a clear ROI can lead to cash flow problems, financial instability, and unsustainable growth, ultimately jeopardising the startup's viability. It can deplete cash reserves, strain financial stability, and increase the startup's dependency on external funding.

Rapid scaling without proper cost control, revenue generation, or profitability can lead to unsustainable growth, cash flow problems, and, ultimately, business failure. Develop a realistic budget and financial plan that aligns with the startup's strategic goals, revenue projections, and funding constraints.

Prioritise investments in areas that drive value creation, such as product development, customer acquisition, and marketing initiatives, while minimising non-essential expenses.

Monitor and analyse key financial metrics, such as burn rate, runway, and cash flow, to ensure financial sustainability and optimise resource allocation.

Additional Tips:

- Adopt a lean startup approach, focusing on efficiency, frugality, and prioritisation of essential expenses to maximise resource utilisation and preserve cash flow.

- Implement robust financial planning, budgeting, and monitoring processes to track expenses, identify cost-saving opportunities, and ensure alignment with strategic priorities.

Change in Regulatory Policies

Regulatory changes or compliance challenges can disrupt operations, increase costs, and create uncertainty, particularly in heavily regulated industries or emerging markets.

Costs and disrupt business operations, particularly in heavily regulated industries or emerging markets.

Failure to anticipate or adapt to regulatory changes may result in non-compliance penalties, legal risks, and reputational damage to the startup. Stay informed about regulatory developments, industry standards, and compliance requirements relevant to your business, proactively monitoring changes and assessing potential impacts.

Establish robust compliance processes, policies, and controls to mitigate regulatory risks and ensure adherence to legal and ethical standards. Diversify market exposure and explore opportunities in less-regulated or more stable jurisdictions to reduce dependency on specific regulatory environments. Regulatory changes or compliance challenges can create uncertainty and increase compliance.

Additional Tips:

- Stay proactive and vigilant in monitoring regulatory developments, policy changes, and compliance requirements relevant to your industry, geography, and business operations.

- Maintain open communication channels with regulatory authorities, seek legal counsel, and invest in compliance training and resources to ensure adherence to applicable laws and regulations.

Inappropriate Investor / Tiff with Investors

Partnering with the wrong investors or experiencing conflicts with investors can lead to misalignment of interests, loss of trust, and distraction from strategic priorities, hindering the startup's growth and success.

Disagreements or disputes with investors may result from divergent expectations, communication breakdowns, or perceived breaches of trust, compromising the startup's ability to secure support, guidance, and resources from investors.

Conduct due diligence on potential investors to assess their track record, investment thesis, and alignment with your startup's goals, values, and culture. Establish clear expectations, communication channels, and reporting mechanisms with investors to develop transparency, accountability, and mutual respect. Address conflicts or disagreements with investors promptly and constructively, seeking to find common ground and resolve issues through open dialogue and negotiation.

Additional Tips:

- Conduct due diligence on potential investors, assessing their investment thesis, track record, and alignment with your startup's goals, values, and growth trajectory.

- Establish clear expectations, communication protocols, and reporting mechanisms with investors from the outset, developing transparency, accountability, and mutual understanding.

- Address conflicts or disagreements with investors promptly and professionally, seeking to resolve issues through open dialogue, negotiation, and compromise to preserve the relationship and mutual benefit.

Developing Cold Feet

Losing confidence or motivation in pursuing the startup venture can result in indecision, procrastination, and missed opportunities, ultimately leading to stagnation or failure. Stay committed to your vision, mission, and long-term goals, maintaining a resilient and determined mindset in the face of challenges and setbacks.

Seek support from mentors, advisers, or peer networks to gain perspective, encouragement, and practical guidance in overcoming doubts or uncertainties.

Break down big goals into smaller, achievable milestones, celebrating progress and successes along the way to stay motivated and focused on moving forward. Losing confidence or motivation in pursuing a startup venture can result from setbacks, challenges, or self-doubt, leading to indecision, procrastination, and missed opportunities.

Fear of failure, rejection, or criticism may contribute to hesitancy, reluctance to take risks, and reluctance to make decisions, hindering progress and innovation.

Additional Tips:

- Meet mentors and family members more often to seek their help and support.
- Talk to the startup community more often.

HANDLING TOUGH SITUATIONS

Embarking on the journey of entrepreneurship is an exhilarating yet challenging endeavour filled with uncertainty, risk, and opportunity. The startup journey is fraught with challenges, uWncertainties, and unexpected obstacles that can test the resilience and adaptability of entrepreneurs.

From navigating market fluctuations and competitive pressures to managing internal conflicts and financial constraints, startups must be prepared to tackle tough situations head-on with creativity, agility, and strategic foresight. This detailed document explores a range of solutions and strategies for handling tough situations throughout the startup life cycle, offering insights and recommendations to empower founders and leaders to overcome adversity and emerge stronger than ever.

ACTION ORIENTED

Pivoting

Pivoting in the context of startups refers to the strategic shift in the company's business model, product, or target market in response to changing market conditions, customer feedback, or other internal or external factors. It involves making significant changes to the company's direction to better align with emerging opportunities or to address challenges.

You have to remain agile and adaptable for successful pivoting. Startups often operate in highly uncertain and dynamic environments where market conditions can change rapidly. By staying agile, you can quickly recognise when adjustments to your strategy are needed and can pivot effectively to capitalise on new opportunities or address emerging challenges.

Pivoting allows startups to:

- Stay relevant in a constantly evolving market.

- Address changing customer needs and preferences.

- Seize new opportunities for growth.

- Overcome obstacles and challenges more effectively.

Ultimately, the ability to pivot strategically and with agility is crucial for startups to navigate the complexities of the business world and to increase their chances of long-term success.

Recognise Signs of Market Feedback

Keep a close eye on various sources of market feedback, such as customer reviews, sales data, social media mentions, and industry reports.

Establish regular feedback loops with customers through surveys, interviews, and focus groups.

Example: A software company notices a decline in user engagement with a particular feature of its product through analytics data and an increase in customer support tickets related to another feature. This signals a need to pivot the product strategy to better align with customer needs and preferences.

Conduct Thorough Market Research and Feasibility Analysis

Gather comprehensive data on market trends, competitor activities, consumer behaviour, and emerging technologies.

Validate assumptions through customer feedback, market testing, and prototype development.

Example: A food delivery service conducts market research and identifies a growing demand for healthy, organic food options. They then conduct a feasibility analysis to assess the potential costs, supply chain logistics, and consumer preferences related to adding these options to their menu.

Communicate Transparently with Stakeholders

Clearly communicate the reasons for pivoting and the vision for the future with all stakeholders, including employees, investors, and customers.

Provide regular updates on the progress of the pivot and any changes to the business strategy.

Example: A retail company communicates with its employees about the need to pivot its sales strategy from in-store to online due to changing consumer preferences and the impact of the COVID-19 pandemic. They also reassure investors about their long-term vision and commitment to adapting to market changes.

Monitor Key Performance Indicators (KPIs) and Customer Feedback

Establish relevant KPIs related to sales, customer acquisition, customer satisfaction, and market share.

Implement systems to regularly track and analyse KPIs and customer feedback.

Example: An e-commerce company closely monitors website traffic, conversion rates, average order value, and customer reviews to identify any shifts in customer behaviour or preferences. They also use tools like Net Promoter Score (NPS) surveys to gauge customer satisfaction and loyalty.

Conduct Scenario Planning and Feasibility Studies

Assess the potential impact of different pivot strategies on revenue, costs, market positioning, and long-term sustainability.

Conduct thorough feasibility studies to evaluate the practicality and feasibility of each pivot option.

Example: A software-as-a-service (SaaS) company conducts scenario planning to assess the impact of pivoting from a subscription-based model to a freemium model. They analyse potential revenue streams, user acquisition costs, customer retention rates, and the competitive landscape to determine the feasibility of the pivot.

Iterate Rapidly and Experiment with Lean Startup Principles

Embrace a culture of experimentation and learning, and be willing to iterate rapidly based on feedback and data.

Implement lean startup principles and agile methodologies to test hypotheses and validate assumptions.

Example: A technology startup uses A/B testing to experiment with different pricing strategies for its product. They gather data on customer response to each pricing option and use this information to refine their pricing strategy and maximise revenue.

By following these steps and remaining adaptable to change, businesses can effectively pivot their strategies to meet evolving market demands and ensure long-term success. Regularly reassessing market conditions, gathering feedback from stakeholders, and being willing to make strategic adjustments are key to staying competitive and thriving in today's dynamic business environment.

Strategic Downsizing

In the dynamic world of startups, downsizing can sometimes become a necessary step for optimising operations and ensuring long-term sustainability. When faced with the need to downsize, you must approach the process strategically and empathetically to minimise the impact on employees and the organisation as a whole. Given below is a detailed guide on how startups can navigate downsizing effectively:

Assess Organisational Structure and Efficiency

Start by conducting a comprehensive assessment of the organisation's structure, resource allocation, and operational efficiency.

Identify areas for optimisation and streamlining, such as redundant processes, overlapping roles, or inefficient workflows.

Example: A tech startup conducts a thorough review of its operations, including its development, marketing, and administrative functions. Through this assessment, the company identifies redundant processes and overlapping roles within the organisation, leading to inefficiencies and increased costs.

Prioritise Critical Roles and Functions

Prioritise roles and functions critical to the core business objectives, considering factors such as skill sets, performance, and strategic alignment.

Identify key roles and functions that directly contribute to the startup's mission, goals, and competitive advantage.

Example: A software development startup identifies software engineers, product managers, and data analysts as critical roles essential for achieving its long-term goals. These roles are directly aligned with the company's product development and innovation strategies.

Support Affected Employees

Provide support and assistance to affected employees through transparent communication, severance packages, and outplacement services.

Communicate openly and honestly with employees about the need for downsizing, the reasons behind the decision, and the potential impact on individuals and the organisation.

Example: A startup conducts individual or group meetings with affected employees to communicate the decision to downsize. During these meetings, the company provides clear and transparent information about severance packages, benefits, and outplacement services available to support employees through the transition. This may include career counselling, resume writing assistance, job search support, and access to networking opportunities.

Conduct Skills Assessment and Talent Audit

Conduct a skills assessment and talent audit to identify core competencies and critical roles needed to support the startup's strategic objectives.

Evaluate the skills, experience, and capabilities of existing employees to determine their suitability for critical roles within the organisation.

Example: A marketing startup conducts a talent audit to identify key skills such as digital marketing expertise, content creation, analytics capabilities, and project management skills. Through this assessment, the company identifies gaps in its current talent pool and areas where additional expertise or resources may be needed to support its strategic objectives.

Offer Retraining and Upskilling Support

Provide support and resources for retraining, upskilling, or reskilling employees affected by downsizing to enhance employability and career transition opportunities.

Offer training programmes, workshops, and educational opportunities to help employees develop new skills or certifications relevant to their career goals.

Example: A startup offers financial assistance for employees to enrol in online courses, attend workshops, or pursue certifications in areas such as project management, digital marketing, data analysis, or software development. By investing in the professional development of its employees, the company not only supports their career transition but also enhances its own talent pool and capabilities.

Communicate Transparently and Empathetically

Communicate transparently and empathetically with remaining employees about the reasons for downsizing, emphasising the long-term vision and commitment to organisational sustainability.

Address any concerns or questions from employees openly and honestly, providing reassurance and support during a period of change and uncertainty.

Example: A startup holds open and honest discussions with remaining employees, providing regular updates and information about the reasons for downsizing, the impact on the organisation, and the steps being taken to support employees through the transition. By developing a culture of transparency and empathy, the company maintains employee morale and engagement, even during challenging times.

By following these steps and approaches, startups can navigate downsizing with empathy and strategic foresight, ensuring minimal disruption to operations and maintaining employee morale and engagement during challenging times. Effective downsizing can ultimately contribute to the startup's ability to adapt, grow, and achieve its long-term goals in a competitive market environment.

Re-aligning

In the ever-changing scenarios of global startups, it is important to remain nimble to adapt and realign, which is essential for long-term success to remain competitive and agile:

Evaluate your Startup's Goals, Priorities, and Market Positioning

Begin by conducting a comprehensive evaluation of your startup's goals, priorities, and market positioning.

Assess whether your current strategies and objectives are still aligned with changing market dynamics and your long-term strategic vision.

Example: A software startup evaluates its goals and market positioning in light of emerging technology trends and customer feedback. They identify the need to shift their focus from traditional software sales to a subscription-based model to better meet customer demands and remain competitive.

Engage Stakeholders in a Collaborative Process

Engage stakeholders, including employees, investors, and customers, in a collaborative process to realign organisational strategies, resources, and processes.

Develop open dialogue and encourage stakeholders to share their insights, concerns, and suggestions for improvement.

Example: A fintech startup holds strategic planning sessions with key stakeholders to discuss emerging challenges and opportunities in the financial services industry. Together, they identify areas for improvement and develop a shared vision for the company's future direction.

Implement Clear Communication Channels and Performance Metrics

Implement clear communication channels and performance metrics to monitor progress and ensure accountability throughout the realignment process.

Keep stakeholders informed about the realignment process, including the goals, objectives, and timelines for implementation.

Example: A healthcare startup establishes regular progress meetings and uses key performance indicators (KPIs) to track the success of its realignment efforts. They provide regular updates to employees, investors, and customers to ensure transparency and accountability.

Engage Employees, Customers, and Other Stakeholders

Engage employees, customers, and other stakeholders in a collaborative process to gather insights, identify pain points, and co-create solutions for realignment.

Leverage feedback from stakeholders to identify areas for improvement and develop strategies to address emerging challenges and opportunities.

Example: A retail startup conducts focus groups and customer surveys to gather feedback on its products, services, and customer experience. They use this feedback to identify areas for improvement and develop new strategies to better meet customer needs and preferences.

Develop a Culture of Innovation and Adaptability

Develop a culture of innovation and adaptability, encouraging experimentation, feedback, and continuous improvement across all levels of the organisation.

Empower employees to take risks, experiment with new ideas, and learn from failure.

Example: A tech startup establishes a "sandbox" environment where employees can experiment with new technologies and ideas. They encourage a culture of innovation by rewarding employees for taking calculated risks and thinking outside the box.

Develop a Roadmap and Action Plan for Realignment

Develop a roadmap and action plan for realignment, setting clear objectives, milestones, and performance metrics to track progress and ensure accountability.

Break down the realignment process into manageable tasks and assign responsibilities to individuals or teams.

Example: A renewable energy startup develops a detailed action plan for transitioning to sustainable manufacturing practices. They set clear objectives, such as reducing carbon emissions and waste, and establish milestones to track progress towards their sustainability goals.

By following these steps and approaches, you can successfully realign your startup's operations, strategies, and goals to ensure they remain competitive, innovative, and responsive to changing market dynamics. Realignment is not just about making incremental changes; it is about rethinking your startup's approach to remain relevant and successful in a rapidly evolving business landscape.

Cost-Cutting

In the competitive landscape of startups, optimising costs is crucial for achieving sustainable growth and long-term success. By implementing strategic cost-cutting measures, startups can improve their financial health, increase profitability, and position themselves for future success. These are some tips on how your startup can effectively cut costs while maintaining operational efficiency:

Conduct a Comprehensive Expense Review

Start by conducting a comprehensive review of expenses, identifying non-essential costs, inefficiencies, and areas for optimisation.

Example: Startup X conducts a detailed analysis of its expenses and identifies areas such as office rent, software subscriptions, and marketing expenses as potential areas for cost reduction.

Implement Cost-Saving Measures

Implement cost-saving measures such as renegotiating contracts, reducing discretionary spending, and optimising resource utilisation.

Example: Startup Y renegotiates its office lease agreement, reducing rental costs by moving to a smaller office space. Additionally, they cut down on non-essential travel and entertainment expenses to further reduce costs.

Prioritise Investments

Prioritise investments that directly contribute to the startup's core business objectives and long-term sustainability.

Example: Startup Z allocates its resources to areas such as product development, customer acquisition, and talent acquisition, which are critical for its growth and expansion.

Outsourcing

Evaluate the feasibility and benefits of outsourcing non-core functions or specialised tasks to external vendors or service providers.

Example: Startup A decides to outsource its accounting and payroll functions to a third-party service provider. By doing so, they can reduce overhead costs and focus on their core business activities.

Selecting Outsourcing Partners

Select outsourcing partners based on criteria such as expertise, reliability, cost-effectiveness, and cultural fit.

Example: Startup B conducts thorough research and selects outsourcing partners that offer high-quality services at competitive prices and align with their company culture and values.

Establish Clear Expectations and Agreements

Establish clear expectations, service level agreements, and communication protocols to ensure seamless collaboration and quality outcomes.

Example: Startup C defines clear deliverables, timelines, and communication channels with its outsourcing partners to ensure that expectations are met and projects are delivered on time and within budget.

Prioritise Cost-Cutting Initiatives

Prioritise cost-cutting initiatives based on their impact on the startup's strategic objectives, revenue generation potential, and long-term sustainability.

Example: Startup D prioritises cost-cutting initiatives that directly impact its bottom line, such as reducing customer acquisition costs and improving operational efficiency.

Consider Alternative Cost-Saving Measures

Consider alternative cost-saving measures such as renegotiating vendor contracts, implementing energy-efficient practices, or optimising supply chain logistics.

Example: Startup E renegotiates its contracts with suppliers to get better rates on raw materials, reducing manufacturing costs and improving profit margins.

Monitor Effectiveness and Adjust Strategies

Monitor the effectiveness of cost-cutting measures through regular financial analysis and reporting, adjusting strategies as needed to achieve desired outcomes without compromising quality or innovation.

Example: Startup F tracks key financial metrics such as operating expenses, gross margins, and cash flow to evaluate the effectiveness of its cost-cutting initiatives. They adjust their strategies as needed to ensure that cost reductions do not compromise product quality or customer satisfaction.

By implementing these cost-cutting strategies, you can optimise your expenses, improve your financial health, and position yourself for sustainable growth and long-term success in the competitive startup ecosystem.

Insourcing

In the quest for sustainable growth and operational efficiency, startups often explore various strategies to optimise costs. One such strategy is insourcing, which involves bringing certain functions or processes in-house to enhance control, flexibility, and efficiency. Here's a detailed guide on how startups can effectively leverage insourcing to optimise costs while maintaining operational excellence:

Assessing Potential Advantages

Start by assessing the potential advantages of bringing certain functions or processes in-house. Consider factors such as control, flexibility, efficiency, and cost-effectiveness.

Example: Startup X, a tech company, assesses the potential advantages of insourcing its software development activities. By bringing development in-house, they can have better control over project timelines, quality, and intellectual property.

Invest in Talent Development and Infrastructure

Invest in talent development, training, and infrastructure to support insourced activities. Develop a culture of innovation and collaboration within the organisation.

Example: Startup Y invests in training programmes and infrastructure to support its insourced customer support function. By developing an in-house skilled and knowledgeable team, they can provide better support to their customers and improve overall service quality.

Striking a Balance

Strike a balance between insourcing and outsourcing based on the startup's strategic objectives, resource constraints, and competitive advantages.

Example: Startup Z decides to insource its marketing and design activities to maintain better control over branding and messaging. However, they continue to outsource non-core functions such as IT support to specialised service providers.

Evaluating Scalability and Strategic Fit

Evaluate the scalability, flexibility, and strategic fit of outsourcing solutions in relation to the startup's growth trajectory, operational requirements, and core competencies.

Example: Startup A evaluates the scalability of its software development needs and determines that insourcing is the best option for long-term growth. By building an in-house development team, they can scale their product development efforts more effectively.

Building Strong Partnerships with Outsourcing Providers

Build strong partnerships with outsourcing providers based on mutual trust, transparency, and shared values. Develop collaboration and innovation in delivering value-added services.

Example: Startup B establishes a strong partnership with its outsourcing provider for IT support. They collaborate closely to ensure seamless integration of services and continuous improvement in IT infrastructure and support.

Establishing Robust Performance Metrics and Governance Mechanisms

Establish robust performance metrics, service level agreements (SLAs), and governance mechanisms to ensure quality, accountability, and compliance with contractual obligations.

Example: Startup C establishes clear performance metrics and SLAs with its outsourcing partners for customer service. Regular performance reviews and governance mechanisms ensure that the outsourced function meets quality standards and customer expectations.

By effectively leveraging insourcing, startups can optimise costs, enhance operational efficiency, and maintain control over critical business functions. By striking the right balance between insourcing and outsourcing and building strong partnerships with outsourcing providers, startups can achieve sustainable growth and long-term success in the competitive startup ecosystem.

Better Sourcing

In an ever-evolving market landscape, businesses need to continually optimise their sourcing strategies to enhance quality, reliability, and cost-effectiveness. To understand the details of better sourcing, adopt these 6 key steps:

Exploring Alternative Sourcing Options

Objective: Improve quality, reliability, and cost-effectiveness by diversifying sourcing options.

Example: A manufacturing company currently relies on a single supplier for a critical component. By exploring alternative suppliers, they can reduce the risk of supply chain disruptions caused by issues such as production delays or quality issues. For instance, they might consider sourcing the component from multiple suppliers or exploring different geographic locations for sourcing.

Utilising Technology and Market Intelligence

Objective: Identify and evaluate potential sourcing partners and opportunities using data-driven insights.

Example: An e-commerce retailer leverages data analytics and market intelligence to identify emerging trends and consumer preferences. By analysing this data, they can identify potential new suppliers or distribution channels that align with market demands, allowing them to stay ahead of the competition.

Establishing Strategic Partnerships and Alliances

Objective: Enhance supply chain resilience and mitigate risks by forming strategic partnerships with suppliers, vendors, and distributors.

Example: A global electronics manufacturer establishes long-term partnerships with key suppliers. By working closely with these suppliers, they can collaborate on product development, improve forecasting accuracy, and implement risk mitigation strategies such as dual sourcing or inventory buffering.

Assessing Total Cost of Ownership (TCO) and Strategic Benefits

Objective: Evaluate the TCO and strategic benefits of insourcing critical functions or processes.

Example: A software development company considers insourcing its customer support function, which is currently outsourced to a third-party service provider. By conducting a TCO analysis, they realised that insourcing would provide greater control over service quality and customer satisfaction, outweighing the initial cost savings associated with outsourcing.

Investing in Infrastructure, Technology, and Talent Development

Objective: Support insourced activities by investing in infrastructure, technology, and talent development to build internal capabilities.

Example: An automotive manufacturer decides to insource its research and development (R&D) department to develop innovation and protect intellectual property. They invest in state-of-the-art technology, such as 3D printing and virtual simulation tools, and provide training programmes to upskill existing employees, enabling them to take on more complex R&D projects.

Continuously Evaluating Operations and Driving Continuous Improvement

Objective: Continuously evaluate the efficiency and effectiveness of insourced operations, benchmarking performance against industry standards and best practices.

Example: A pharmaceutical company regularly reviews its insourced manufacturing processes to identify areas for improvement. By benchmarking their operations against industry standards and best practices, they can implement changes such as process automation or quality control enhancements to drive efficiency and reduce costs.

By following these steps, businesses can optimise their sourcing strategies, enhance supply chain resilience, and drive continuous improvement across their operations.

STRATEGIC DECISIONS ORIENTED

Taking Expert Advice

1. Seek guidance and mentorship from experienced industry professionals, advisers, or subject matter experts to gain insights, perspective, and strategic direction.

2. Build a diverse network of mentors, advisers, and peer groups who can offer specialised knowledge, relevant experience, and constructive feedback.

3. Actively listen to and consider expert advice, weighing the merits and implications before making informed decisions that align with the startup's goals and values.

4. Seek advice and guidance from diverse sources, including industry experts, mentors, advisers, and peer networks, to gain multiple perspectives and insights on complex challenges.

5. Actively engage with experts through networking events, industry conferences, and advisory board meetings, building relationships and tapping into their knowledge, experience, and networks.

6. Exercise discernment and critical thinking when evaluating expert advice, considering the context, credibility, and relevance of the information in relation to the startup's specific goals and challenges.

Taking Tough Decisions

1. Embrace difficult decisions with courage, conviction, and empathy, prioritising the long-term interests and sustainability of the startup.

2. Gather relevant data, insights, and perspectives to inform tough decisions, balancing pragmatism with empathy and ethical considerations.

3. Communicate transparently and authentically with stakeholders about the rationale, process, and implications of tough decisions, developing trust, understanding, and alignment.

4. Develop a decision-making framework or process that incorporates input from multiple stakeholders, data-driven analysis, and ethical considerations to guide tough decisions.

5. Communicate decisively and empathetically with stakeholders about tough decisions, providing context, rationale, and a clear path forward to maintain trust and alignment.

6. Reflect on the outcomes and lessons learned from tough decisions, iterating on decision-making processes and leadership practices to enhance resilience and adaptability in the face of future challenges.

Sale of Business/ Part Sale/ Mergers

Selling a business, part of a business, or entering into a merger is a significant decision for any startup. To ensure a successful transaction that maximises value for stakeholders while safeguarding the interests of employees, customers, and other stakeholders, it is essential to follow a structured and strategic approach.

Assess Feasibility and Strategic Rationale

Evaluate the feasibility and strategic rationale for selling the business, considering factors such as market conditions, valuation, and long-term growth prospects.

Example: A software startup assesses the current market conditions, its growth trajectory, and potential valuation to determine whether selling the business aligns with its long-term strategic objectives.

Engage with Potential Buyers or Investors

Engage with potential buyers or investors through a structured and confidential process to explore acquisition or investment opportunities.

Example: A healthtech startup identifies strategic acquirers and investors through networking, industry events, and targeted outreach. They then initiate discussions with interested parties to explore potential acquisition or investment opportunities.

Negotiate Terms and Conditions

Negotiate terms and conditions that maximise value for stakeholders while safeguarding the interests of employees, customers, and other stakeholders.

Example: A fintech startup negotiates the sale terms with potential buyers, ensuring that key employee benefits, customer contracts, and brand reputation are protected throughout the transaction process.

Conduct Thorough Valuation and Due Diligence

Conduct a thorough valuation and due diligence process to assess the market value, potential buyers, and strategic fit for the sale of the business.

Example: A biotech startup engages financial experts to conduct a comprehensive valuation and due diligence process. This includes assessing the company's intellectual property, financial performance, regulatory compliance, and market positioning to determine its market value and attractiveness to potential buyers.

Engage with Experienced M&A Advisers

Engage with experienced M&A advisers, legal counsel, and financial experts to navigate the complexities of the sale process and maximise value for stakeholders.

Example: A SaaS startup hires an experienced M&A advisory firm to manage the sale process. The advisory firm provides strategic guidance, conducts negotiations on behalf of the startup, and ensures that the transaction is structured to maximise value and mitigate risks.

Consider Alternative Exit Strategies

Consider alternative exit strategies, such as mergers, acquisitions, or strategic partnerships, to achieve business objectives and unlock value while preserving your startup's legacy and mission.

Example: A renewable energy startup explores alternative exit strategies, including mergers with larger industry players or strategic partnerships with established energy companies. This allows the startup to achieve its growth objectives while preserving its commitment to sustainability and innovation.

By following these steps and approaches, startups can navigate the sale process effectively, maximise value for stakeholders, and achieve their long-term strategic objectives. Whether selling the entire business, part of the business, or entering into a merger, a structured and strategic approach is essential for a successful transaction that preserves the startup's legacy and mission.

UNDERSTANDING THE SUNK COSTS PHENOMENON

In the dynamic and often uncertain world of startups, making strategic decisions is crucial for success. One essential concept that, as a founder and entrepreneur, you need to understand is "sunk costs."

Sunk costs refer to the money, time, and resources that have already been invested in a project or endeavour and cannot be recovered, regardless of future outcomes. In other words, a sunk cost is a cost that has already been incurred and cannot be recovered, no matter what decision is made moving forward.

Importance of Understanding Sunk Costs

Understanding sunk costs is essential for startups because it helps founders and entrepreneurs make better strategic decisions. By recognising that sunk costs are irrelevant to future decisions, startups can avoid falling into the trap of throwing good money after bad and instead focus on maximising future value and returns.

Examples of Sunk Costs in Startups:

Investments in Product Development

Example: A software startup has invested significant time and resources in developing a new mobile app. However, after beta testing, they realise that there is little demand for the app and that it does not meet the needs of their target market.

Despite the sunk costs associated with the development of the app, the startup decides to pivot and focus on a new product that has better market potential. Although the time and resources invested in developing the app are considered sunk costs, the startup understands that continuing to invest in a product with limited market potential would only lead to further losses.

Marketing and Advertising Expenses

Example: A fashion startup has spent a substantial amount of money on a marketing campaign to promote a new clothing line. However, after analysing the results of the campaign, they determine that it did not generate the expected level of sales.

Despite the sunk costs associated with the marketing campaign, the startup decides to shift its marketing strategy and focus on different channels or target demographics.

Even though the money spent on the marketing campaign is considered a sunk cost, the startup realises that continuing with the same strategy would not lead to the desired results, making it more beneficial to reallocate resources to other marketing initiatives.

Hiring and Training Costs

Example: A tech startup has hired and trained a team of engineers to develop a new software product. However, after several months of development, they realise that the product is not meeting customer expectations and that there are significant technical challenges that cannot be overcome.

Despite the sunk costs associated with hiring and training the engineering team, the startup decided to halt development on the product and reallocate resources to other projects. While the money and time invested in hiring and training the engineering team are considered sunk costs, the startup understands that continuing to invest in a product with limited potential would only lead to further losses.

Decision-Making Considering Sunk Costs

Focus on Future Costs and Benefits

When making strategic decisions, focus on future costs and benefits rather than past investments.

Example: Instead of considering the money already spent on product development, focus on the potential revenue and market opportunities associated with different product options. By focusing on future costs and benefits, startups can make more informed decisions that maximise future value and returns.

Evaluate Alternatives Objectively

Evaluate all available alternatives objectively, considering their potential costs, benefits, risks, and opportunities.

Example: Compare the potential returns and market opportunities associated with different product options, regardless of the sunk costs associated with each option. By evaluating alternatives objectively, startups can identify the best course of action moving forward.

Learn from Past Mistakes

Use the lessons learned from past investments and failures to inform future decisions and strategies.

Example: Analyse the reasons why previous investments did not generate the expected returns and use this information to make better decisions in the future. By learning from past mistakes, startups can avoid repeating the same errors and make more strategic decisions that drive long-term success.

Understanding sunk costs is essential for startups because it helps founders and entrepreneurs make better strategic decisions. By focusing on future costs and benefits, evaluating alternatives objectively, and learning from past mistakes, startups can avoid falling into the trap of sunk cost fallacy and instead focus on maximising future value and returns.

By making informed decisions that prioritise future potential over past investments, startups can navigate the challenges of the startup journey more effectively and increase their chances of long-term success.

THE STARTUP ECOSYSTEM

In this chapter, we dive into the key features of India's startup ecosystem, highlight notable unicorns, discuss prominent funding agencies, explore compliance requirements, and elucidate the government's support mechanisms for startups.

THE INDIAN STARTUP ECOSYSTEM

India has emerged as one of the most vibrant and dynamic startup ecosystems globally. With a myriad of opportunities across diverse sectors, the Indian startup landscape has witnessed unprecedented growth in recent years. The government initiatives, such as "Startup India," have provided a conducive environment for entrepreneurs to flourish.

Various sectors, including technology, healthcare, and renewable energy, have seen a surge in innovative startups aiming to address unique challenges in the Indian context.

Navigating the Indian startup ecosystem involves understanding the regulatory framework, funding landscape, and cultural nuances. This chapter serves as a comprehensive introduction, offering insights into the current state of the ecosystem and preparing founders for the exciting yet challenging journey of building a startup in India.

India's startup ecosystem has undergone a remarkable transformation in recent years, evolving into one of the most dynamic and thriving hubs for innovation and entrepreneurship globally. With a burgeoning young population, robust technological infrastructure, and a supportive regulatory environment, India offers a fertile ground for startups across various sectors to flourish and scale.

Features of India's Startup Ecosystem

India's startup ecosystem boasts several distinctive features that contribute to its vibrancy and attractiveness to entrepreneurs:

Large Domestic Market

India's vast and diverse domestic market provides startups with ample opportunities for market penetration and scalability across sectors such as technology, e-commerce, healthcare, and finance.

Tech Talent Pool

India is home to a vast pool of skilled technical talent, including engineers, developers, and data scientists, nurtured by premier educational institutions and a thriving IT industry.

Growing Investor Interest

The increasing appetite of domestic and international investors for Indian startups has led to a surge in funding across various stages, developing innovation and growth.

Supportive Policies

The Indian government has implemented several initiatives and policy reforms to promote entrepreneurship, ease regulatory compliance, and facilitate access to funding and infrastructure for startups.

Startup Hubs

Cities like Bangalore, Mumbai, Delhi-NCR, Hyderabad, and Pune have emerged as vibrant startup hubs, offering a conducive ecosystem comprising co-working spaces, incubators, accelerators, and networking opportunities.

Unicorns in India

India boasts a burgeoning list of unicorns—startups valued at over \$1 billion—across diverse sectors. Notable unicorns include Flipkart (e-commerce), Paytm (fintech), Ola (ride-hailing), Byju's (edtech), Zomato (food delivery), and Oyo (hospitality). These unicorns serve as beacons of success, inspiring aspiring entrepreneurs and highlighting the potential for exponential growth within India's startup ecosystem.

Nodal Agency for Startup Promotion and Policy Making

The Department for Promotion of Industry and Internal Trade (DPIIT) is the nodal agency of the Government of India for promotion and policy-making for startups in India. It plays a pivotal role in germinating the growth and development of startups in India. As the nodal agency for formulating and implementing policies related to industrial promotion and entrepreneurship, DPIIT is instrumental in creating a conducive environment for startups to thrive. Its initiatives, such as Startup India, aim to streamline regulatory processes, provide access to funding and infrastructure, offer mentorship and networking opportunities, and facilitate ease of doing business for startups.

DPIIT is support is crucial for startups at various stages of their journey, from inception to scale-up, as it helps address regulatory hurdles, promotes innovation, and encourages entrepreneurial spirit across diverse sectors. By championing the interests of startups and facilitating their integration into the broader economy, DPIIT plays a significant role in driving India's entrepreneurial ecosystem forward and germinating economic growth and job creation.

Compliance Agencies and Benefits

While navigating the regulatory landscape is essential for startups, compliance requirements can sometimes be daunting. Key compliance agencies and benefits for startups include:

1. Ministry of Corporate Affairs (MCA)

Responsible for regulating corporate affairs in India, MCA oversees compliance requirements related to company registration, corporate governance, and annual filings.

2. Goods and Services Tax (GST)

Startups need to comply with GST regulations for tax registration, filing returns, and maintaining records, benefiting from simplified compliance procedures for small businesses.

3. Intellectual Property India (IPI)

IPI facilitates the registration and protection of intellectual property rights, including patents, trademarks, and copyrights, crucial for safeguarding innovations and developing innovation-driven entrepreneurship.

4. Startup India Initiative

Launched by the Government of India, Startup India offers several benefits and incentives to startups, including tax exemptions, fast-track patent examination, funding support, and access to incubation and mentorship programmes.

5. SEBI (Securities and Exchange Board of India)

SEBI regulates the securities market in India and oversees compliance requirements for startups seeking to raise funds through avenues such as IPOs (Initial Public Offerings) or private placements.

India's startup ecosystem embodies a potent blend of innovation, opportunity, and support, offering a fertile ground for entrepreneurs to transform ideas into scalable businesses. With a conducive regulatory environment, robust funding ecosystem, and government backing, startups at various stages can thrive and contribute to India's economic growth and technological advancement. By leveraging the resources and support available within the ecosystem, startups can navigate challenges, achieve sustainable growth, and realise their aspirations of making a meaningful impact on society.

Support Services and Growth Facilitation

India has several startup promotion bodies and initiatives aimed at developing entrepreneurship, providing support services, and facilitating growth opportunities for startups. These are some notable ones:

1. Startup India

Launched by the Government of India in 2016, Startup India is a flagship initiative aimed at promoting and supporting startups across the country. It offers various benefits and incentives, including tax exemptions, fast-track patent examination, funding support, and access to incubation centres and mentorship programmes. Startup India also provides an online platform for startups to register, access resources, and connect with stakeholders.

2. NASSCOM 10,000 Startups

NASSCOM 10,000 Startups is an initiative by the National Association of Software and Service Companies (NASSCOM) aimed at giving rise to the growth of 10,000 technology startups in India by providing access to resources, mentoring, networking opportunities, and market connect programmes. It offers a range of initiatives, including acceleration programmes, startup showcases, and industry partnerships, to support early-stage and growth-stage startups in the technology sector.

3. Indian Angel Network (IAN)

Indian Angel Network is one of the largest angel investor networks in India, comprising successful entrepreneurs, industry experts, and high-net-worth individuals (HNIs). IAN provides funding, mentorship, and strategic support to early-stage startups across various sectors, helping them scale and succeed in the market.

4. TiE (The Indus Entrepreneurs)

TiE is a global nonprofit organisation focused on developing entrepreneurship through mentoring, networking, and education. TiE chapters in India, including TiE Delhi-NCR, TiE Bangalore, and TiE Mumbai, offer programmes and events aimed at nurturing startups, connecting them with investors, and facilitating knowledge sharing among entrepreneurs.

5. State Startup Policy Initiatives

Several Indian states have launched startup policies and initiatives to promote entrepreneurship and innovation within their respective regions. For example, states like Karnataka, Telangana, Maharashtra, and Gujarat have established startup promotion bodies, incubation centres, and funding schemes to support startups and create conducive ecosystems for entrepreneurship.

6. Atal Innovation Mission (AIM)

AIM is a flagship initiative by the Government of India aimed at promoting innovation and entrepreneurship among students, entrepreneurs, and researchers. It operates through various programmes, including Atal Incubation Centres (AICs), Atal Tinkering Labs (ATLs) in schools, Atal New India Challenges (ANIC), and Atal Community Innovation Centres (ACICs), to develop innovation and create a culture of entrepreneurship across the country.

These startup promotion bodies and initiatives play a crucial role in providing support, guidance, and resources to startups at different stages of their journey, contributing to the growth and success of India's vibrant startup ecosystem.

Key Funding Agencies

Several funding agencies play a pivotal role in supporting startups at various stages of their journey. Some prominent ones include:

1. Venture Capital Firms

Venture capital firms such as Sequoia Capital India, Accel Partners, Nexus Venture Partners, and Lightspeed India Partners provide seed, early-stage, and growth capital to promising startups, along with strategic guidance and industry connections.

2. Angel Investors

Angel investors, including successful entrepreneurs, corporate executives, and HNIs (High-Net-Worth Individuals), often invest in early-stage startups, offering not just financial support but also mentorship and access to networks.

3. Government Initiatives

Government-backed entities such as the Small Industries Development Bank of India (SIDBI), National Small Industries Corporation (NSIC), and various state-level startup funds provide financial assistance, loan guarantees, and other support services to startups.

4. Corporate Venture Capital (CVC)

Many corporates have established venture capital arms to invest in startups relevant to their industry verticals, developing innovation and potential strategic partnerships.

Grants and Funding Support

Grants and funding support from both government and private organisations play a significant role in promoting and nurturing startups. Here's an overview of various grants and funding opportunities available for startups in India:

1. Startup India Seed Fund Scheme

Launched by the Government of India, this scheme provides financial assistance to startups for proof of concept, prototype development, product trials, market entry, and commercialisation. Startups can receive up to INR 20 lakhs in funding under this scheme.

2. Technology Business Incubators (TBIs)

TBIs supported by the Department of Science and Technology (DST) provide financial assistance, infrastructure, mentoring, and other support services to startups in specific technology sectors, including biotechnology, ICT, and clean energy.

3. Biotechnology Ignition Grant (BIG)

Offered by the Biotechnology Industry Research Assistance Council (BIRAC), BIG provides early-stage funding to startups and entrepreneurs in the biotechnology sector. It supports proof of concept, prototype development, and validation of innovative biotech ideas.

4. Atal Innovation Mission (AIM) Grants

AIM provides various grants and funding opportunities to promote innovation and entrepreneurship, including Atal New India Challenges (ANIC), Atal Incubation Centres (AICs), and Atal Community Innovation Centres (ACICs), among others.

5. Millennium Alliance (MA)

Millennium Alliance, a partnership between the Government of India, the United States Agency for International Development (USAID), and other stakeholders provides funding and support to startups with innovative solutions in sectors such as agriculture, healthcare, clean energy, and water.

6. MSME Schemes

The Ministry of Micro, Small, and Medium Enterprises (MSME) offers several schemes and programmes to support startups and small businesses, including the Credit Guarantee Fund Scheme, Scheme of Fund for Regeneration of Traditional Industries (SFURTI), and Technology and Quality Upgradation Support to MSMEs.

7. Private Grants and Funding

Venture Capital Funding: Venture capital firms such as Sequoia Capital, Accel Partners, and Lightspeed Venture Partners provide funding to startups at various stages of growth, from seed funding to series rounds. These firms also offer mentorship, networking, and strategic guidance to portfolio companies.

8. National Research Development Corporation (NRDC) Grants

NRDC offers financial assistance, technology commercialisation support, and access to infrastructure and expertise to startups and MSMEs for the development and commercialisation of indigenous technologies.

9. Credit Guarantee Fund Scheme for Startups (CGFS)

Launched by the Ministry of Micro, Small and Medium Enterprises (MSME), CGFS provides collateral-free credit facilities to startups to meet working capital requirements and acquire machinery or equipment. The scheme enables startups to access loans from banks and financial institutions without the need for collateral security.

10. NIDHI Prayas Grant

NIDHI Prayas, an initiative under the National Initiative for Development and Harnessing Innovations (NIDHI), provides financial support of up to INR 10 lakhs to startups for prototyping, testing, and validation of innovative ideas or technologies.

11. Angel Investor Networks

Angel investor networks like Indian Angel Network (IAN), Mumbai Angels, and Chennai Angels invest in early-stage startups and provide funding, mentorship, and industry connections to entrepreneurs.

12. Corporate Accelerator Programmes

Many corporates run accelerator programmes and innovation challenges to support startups working on solutions relevant to their industry verticals. These programmes often provide funding, mentorship, access to resources, and potential pilot opportunities with corporate partners.

13. Incubator and Accelerator Programmes

Private incubators and accelerators, such as IKP Eden, NSRCEL in India and Y Combinator (US), offer funding, mentorship, and resources to startups in exchange for equity. These programmes typically provide intensive support to help startups scale and succeed.

14. Crowdfunding Platforms

Crowdfunding Platforms enable startups to raise funds from a large number of individuals or investors through crowdfunding campaigns. Startups pitch their ideas or products to the public, who can then contribute funds in exchange for rewards or equity.

15. Corporate Social Responsibility (CSR) Funding

Many corporates allocate funds for CSR activities, including support for startups and social enterprises. Startups working on solutions aligned with a corporate's CSR objectives may receive grants or funding support for their initiatives.

16. Grant Challenges and Competitions

Various organisations, foundations, and non-profits organise grant challenges and competitions to identify and fund innovative startups addressing specific social or environmental challenges. Examples include the Tata Social Enterprise Challenge, Villgro Innovation Challenge, and DBS-NUS Social Venture Challenge Asia.

17. Startup Competitions and Accelerator Programmes

Startup competitions and accelerator programmes, such as the Google for Startups Accelerator, Microsoft for Startups, and AWS Activate, provide funding, mentorship, and resources to startups selected for their programmes.

18. Sector-Specific Grants and Funds

Several private organisations and foundations offer sector-specific grants and funds to startups operating in areas such as education, healthcare, agriculture, and clean energy. These grants may support research and development, pilot projects, or market expansion initiatives.

19. Impact Investors and Venture Philanthropists

Impact investors and venture philanthropists invest in startups and social enterprises with the dual objective of generating financial returns and creating positive social or environmental impact. They may provide grants, equity investments, or debt financing to startups aligned with their impact objectives.

20. Startup Grind

Startup Grind is a global community of entrepreneurs, founders, and innovators that hosts events, workshops, and networking sessions to connect startup enthusiasts and develop collaboration. With chapters in major cities across India, Startup Grind provides a platform for startups to learn from successful entrepreneurs, share experiences, and access valuable resources.

21. TiE (The Indus Entrepreneurs)

TiE is a nonprofit organisation dedicated to developing entrepreneurship through mentoring, networking, and education. TiE chapters in India organise various events, workshops, and mentorship programmes to support startups at different stages of their journey. TiE also facilitates connections with investors, industry experts, and other stakeholders in the startup ecosystem.

22. Indian Angel Network (IAN)

Indian Angel Network is one of the largest angel investor networks in India, comprising successful entrepreneurs, industry leaders, and HNIs (High-Net-Worth Individuals). Apart from providing funding, IAN offers mentorship, strategic guidance, and networking opportunities to early-stage startups, helping them navigate challenges and scale their businesses.

23. NASSCOM 10,000 Startups

NASSCOM 10,000 Startups is an initiative by the National Association of Software and Service Companies (NASSCOM) aimed at developing the growth of technology startups in India. It provides access to mentorship, networking, and funding opportunities, along with industry partnerships and market connect programmes.

24. FICCI (Federation of Indian Chambers of Commerce and Industry)

FICCI is one of the largest and oldest industry associations in India, representing the interests of businesses across various sectors. FICCI's startup initiatives include organising conferences, seminars, and policy dialogues to address challenges faced by startups and advocate for conducive policies and regulatory reforms.

25. CII (Confederation of Indian Industry)

CII is another prominent industry association in India that supports startups and entrepreneurship through its various initiatives, including startup summits, workshops, and knowledge sharing platforms. CII collaborates with government agencies, corporates, and other stakeholders to create an enabling environment for startups to thrive.

26. ASSOCHAM (The Associated Chambers of Commerce and Industry of India)

ASSOCHAM is a leading industry body that promotes trade and commerce in India. It organises events, seminars, and business conferences to facilitate interactions between startups, investors, and industry players, developing partnerships and collaboration opportunities.

27. Headstart

Headstart Network Foundation is a prominent grassroots-level organisation in India that is dedicated to developing entrepreneurship and promoting startup culture. It operates through a network of local chapters in cities such as Bangalore, Mumbai, Delhi-NCR, Pune, Hyderabad, Chennai, and Kolkata. Each chapter organises regular events, workshops, and mentorship sessions tailored to the needs of the local startup community. Headstart chapters provide startups with access to resources, mentorship, and opportunities to showcase their products or services.

These self-help groups, private bodies, and associations serve as valuable platforms for startups to connect with peers, mentors, investors, and industry experts, enabling them to access resources, gain insights, and navigate the challenges of entrepreneurship more effectively.

By leveraging these government and private grants and funding options, startups can access the financial resources and support they need to accelerate their growth, scale their impact, and drive innovation across diverse sectors in India.

BENEFITS TO STARTUPS IN INDIA

Startups in India can avail themselves of several incentives and benefits provided by the government to encourage entrepreneurship and innovation. These incentives are aimed at easing regulatory compliance, providing financial support, and developing a conducive ecosystem for startups to thrive. Here are some key incentives and benefits available to startups in India:

1. Startup India Recognition and Certification

Startups recognised by the Department for Promotion of Industry and Internal Trade (DPIIT) under the Startup India initiative are eligible for various benefits, including self-certification under labour and environmental laws, easier winding up of companies, and access to government procurement opportunities.

2. Tax Benefits

Startups registered under the Startup India initiative are eligible for income tax exemptions for the first 3 consecutive years of operation. Additionally, they are exempt from the 'Angel Tax' on investments received from angel investors up to a certain threshold.

3. Fast-track Patent Examination

Startups can avail themselves of expedited patent examination under the Startup India initiative, reducing the time taken to obtain patents for their innovative products or processes.

4. Funding Support

Various government schemes, such as the Startup India Seed Fund Scheme, provide financial assistance to startups for proof of concept, prototype development, and market entry. Additionally, startups can access funding from government-backed entities like SIDBI, BIRAC, and NSIC.

5. Ease of Doing Business

The government has introduced several reforms to improve the ease of doing business for startups, including simplification of company registration procedures, digitalisation of regulatory processes, and reduction in compliance requirements.

6. Infrastructure Support

Startup hubs, incubators, and co-working spaces supported by the government provide startups with access to affordable office space, mentorship, networking opportunities, and other support services.

7. Research and Development Incentives

Startups engaged in research and development (R&D) activities may avail themselves of tax incentives and grants under schemes like the Technology Business Incubator (TBI) programme and the Biotechnology Ignition Grant (BIG) scheme.

8. Access to Markets

Government procurement programmes, such as the Government e-Marketplace (GeM), provide startups with opportunities to supply goods and services to government departments and agencies.

9. International Exposure

The government facilitates participation of startups in international trade fairs, exhibitions, and delegations to showcase their products and explore global markets.

10. Skill Development

The government provides support for skill development and capacity building of startup founders and employees through initiatives like the National Entrepreneurship Development Programme (NEDP) and Skill India Mission.

These incentives and benefits make India an attractive destination for startups, encouraging innovation, job creation, and economic growth. By leveraging these schemes and support mechanisms, startups can overcome challenges, accelerate their growth, and contribute to India's startup ecosystem and economy.

The Indian startup ecosystem is a vibrant and dynamic landscape that offers immense opportunities for innovation, growth, and entrepreneurship. With a supportive regulatory environment, a large domestic market, a thriving tech talent pool, and access to funding and support initiatives, India has emerged as one of the world's leading hubs for startups. Government initiatives like Startup India, coupled with private sector participation and grassroots efforts by organisations like Headstart and TiE, have created a conducive ecosystem for startups to flourish across diverse sectors.

Despite challenges, Indian startups continue to disrupt traditional industries, drive technological advancements, and make significant contributions to economic development and job creation. As the ecosystem evolves and matures, collaboration, innovation, and inclusivity will remain key drivers of success, ensuring that India continues to be at the forefront of global entrepreneurship and innovation.

THE JOURNEY CONTINUES –
YOUR STARTUP'S FUTURE

As we reach the end of this book, it is essential to recognise that this is not just a conclusion—it is a new beginning. The process of raising a startup is far from linear; it is a dynamic, ever-evolving journey filled with challenges, triumphs, learning experiences, and growth. By now, you have learned the principles and strategies to guide you, but the real journey lies ahead.

REFLECT ON YOUR JOURNEY

Take a moment to reflect on how far you have come. Remember the early days when your idea was just a seed—a spark of inspiration fuelled by passion and determination. Think about the countless hours you invested in research, planning, and development. You took the plunge into the unknown, facing obstacles and uncertainties head-on.

You have learned to pivot when necessary, adapting to market changes and customer feedback. You have celebrated the small victories that reminded you why you started this journey in the first place. You have also weathered setbacks and challenges that tested your resolve and forced you to dig deep, finding the strength to keep going. Each step has been a testament to your resilience, creativity, and passion.

As you look back, recognise that every experience—good or bad—has shaped you into the entrepreneur you are today. These experiences have given you valuable insights and have prepared you for the challenges that lie ahead.

BUILDING A SUSTAINABLE FUTURE

As your startup grows, the challenges will evolve. Scaling your operations, managing a larger team, and adapting to market changes will require a new set of skills and strategies. Growth brings complexity, and with it, the need for a solid foundation that can support your expansion.

This is the time to focus on building a sustainable future for your startup. Ensure that your business model is robust, your finances are in order, and your operations are efficient. Develop processes that can scale, and invest in technology that can streamline your operations and enhance productivity.

But beyond the mechanics of growth, remember that the foundation you have built—your vision, values, and the culture you have nurtured—will be the anchor that guides you through the complexities of growth. These elements are the core of your startup's identity, and they will be crucial in maintaining cohesion and purpose as your company expands.

Continue to invest in your people, as they are the heart of your company. A strong, motivated team can make the difference between success and failure. Develop a culture of innovation, where every team member feels empowered to contribute ideas and drive the company forward. Encourage collaboration, celebrate diversity, and create an environment where creativity thrives.

Your leadership will set the tone for the entire organisation. Lead with empathy, transparency, and a commitment to continuous improvement. Be a role model for your team, showing them that success is not just about profits but about creating value, making a difference, and staying true to your principles.

EMBRACE THE UNKNOWN

The future is uncertain, but that is what makes the entrepreneurial journey so exciting. Embrace the unknown with curiosity and confidence. The landscape of business is constantly changing, and what works today may not work tomorrow. Be willing to take calculated risks, experiment with new ideas, and explore uncharted territories.

The most successful startups are those that adapt quickly and learn from both successes and failures. Do not be afraid to make mistakes—what matters is how you respond to them. Each setback is an opportunity to learn, grow, and refine your approach.

Stay connected with your network—mentors, advisers, and fellow entrepreneurs—who can provide valuable insights and support. The entrepreneurial journey can be lonely at times, but you do not have to go it alone. Surround yourself with people who challenge your thinking, offer diverse perspectives, and inspire you to push the boundaries of what is possible.

Keep your ear to the ground, staying informed about industry trends and emerging technologies. Be open to new opportunities that align with your vision, and be ready to pivot when necessary. The ability to anticipate and respond to change will be one of your greatest assets as an entrepreneur.

THE LEGACY YOU ARE BUILDING

Remember, you are not just building a company; you are creating a legacy. The impact of your startup goes beyond profits and market share. You have the opportunity to shape industries, create jobs, and contribute to the well-being of your community.

Consider the broader implications of your work. How is your startup making the world a better place? What values are you promoting through your products, services, and business practices? Your startup is a reflection of your vision for the future, and you have the power to influence not just your industry, but society as a whole.

Keep sight of the bigger picture and the positive change you can bring to the world. As you grow, think about how you can give back—whether it is through corporate social responsibility initiatives, sustainability efforts, or supporting causes that are close to your heart.

Your legacy will also be defined by the way you treat people—your employees, customers, partners, and community. Build relationships based on trust, respect, and mutual benefit. Be known as a company that stands by its principles, delivers on its promises, and values people over profits.

As you move forward, keep asking yourself: What do you want your startup to stand for? How do you want to be remembered as a leader? Let these questions guide your decisions and actions, ensuring that your legacy is one you can be proud of.

KEEP THE FIRE ALIVE

Finally, never lose the passion that brought you here. The startup journey is long and demanding, but it is also one of the most rewarding experiences you can undertake. There will be days when the challenges seem overwhelming, when progress is slow, and when the future feels uncertain. In those moments, remember why you started this journey in the first place.

Keep the fire alive by staying true to your vision and values. Let your passion fuel your determination to overcome obstacles and reach new heights.

Surround yourself with people who share your enthusiasm and can help reignite your motivation when it wanes.

Continue to learn and grow as an entrepreneur. The more you expand your knowledge and skills, the better equipped you'll be to navigate the challenges ahead. Seek out new experiences, be open to feedback, and never stop improving.

Remember, the startup journey is not just about the destination—it is about the process, the learning, and the growth. Celebrate the milestones, but also take the time to enjoy the journey itself. Every step you take, every challenge you overcome, and every lesson you learn is a testament to your growth as an entrepreneur and as a person.

This is not the end. It is the continuation of a story that is uniquely yours. The world is full of possibilities, and your startup has the potential to make a lasting impact. Go forth with confidence, resilience, and the knowledge that you have what it takes to succeed.

Your startup's future is bright, and the best is yet to come.

Signing Off, But Not Goodbye

This book may be coming to an end, but your journey is just beginning. I will be rooting for you every step of the way. Remember, the world needs more daring entrepreneurs like you. Keep pushing forward, and keep raising your startup to new heights.

If you ever need a reminder of how far you have come or a boost of inspiration, return to these pages. The journey of entrepreneurship is ongoing, and every step forward brings new lessons and opportunities.

Thank you for embarking on this journey with me. I wish you every success as you continue to build, innovate, and inspire. And while this is my final chapter in this book, it is only the beginning of your incredible story.

Wishing you all the best on your incredible journey ahead!!

ABOUT THE AUTHOR

 "Dr. Sanjeev Patni is a serial entrepreneur with an experience of launching successful startups and a committed mentor. He has a profound understanding of the complete startup ecosystem, from ideation to scale-up. He is a thought leader in the industry, frequently sought after to share his insights and perspectives on various industry forums.

Driven by a passion for nurturing talent and fostering innovation, he actively engages with startups, providing them with invaluable guidance and mentorship. His hands-on approach, coupled with his experience, enables him to steer budding entrepreneurs on the path to success. His commitment to empowering startups extends beyond mere mentorship; he is deeply invested in their journey, leveraging his network and resources to facilitate their growth and expansion.

He is at the forefront of driving innovation and change, envisioning a future where startups take the centre-stage for innovations and inventions to solve problems, making a lasting impact on the global landscape

He incubates and mentors startups and is dedicated to nurturing valuable startups and shaping them into global forces. His vision is to create an ecosystem that develops entrepreneurship, innovation, and catalyses economic growth. Through his leadership and mentorship, Dr. Patni is committed to empowering the next generation of entrepreneurs, driving forward the startup ecosystem".

dr.sanjeevpatni@gmail.com

www.startupreneur.in

https://www.linkedin.com/company/the-startupreneur/posts/

the_startupreneur